DALE FIERS
Twentieth Century Disciple

❖ ❖ ❖ ❖ ❖ ❖ ❖ *The credit belongs to the man who is actually in the arena, whose face is marred by dust and sweat and blood, who knows the great enthusiasms, the great devotions, and spends himself in a worthy cause; who at best, if he wins, knows the thrills of high achievement, and, if he fails, at least fails daring greatly, so that his place shall never be with those cold and timid souls who know neither victory nor defeat.*

JOHN F. KENNEDY
DECEMBER 5, 1961

DALE FIERS
Twentieth Century Disciple

D. DUANE CUMMINS

TCU PRESS ❖ FORT WORTH

Library of Congress Cataloging-in-Publication Data

Cummins, D. Duane
    Dale Fiers: Twentieth Century Disciple/ by D. Duane Cummins.
        p. cm.
    Includes bibliographical references and index
        ISBN 0-87565-278-6 (cloth : alk. paper)
    1. Fiers, A. Dale (Alan Dale), 1907-   . Christian Church (Disciples
of Christ)— Clergy— Biography   I. Title
BX7343.F53 C86 2003
186.6'092—dc21
                                                                    2003001137

Cover and text design by Bill Maize; Duo Design Group

Cover photo, left to right: Gaines M. Cook, Wilbur C. Parry, Sr.,
Riley B. Montgomery, W. A. Welsh, Loren E. Lair, Hampton Adams,
and John Rogers. Photo courtesy Religious News Service.

Funding for this three-year project was generously provided by Alan Fiers, the
Oreon E. Scott Foundation, and the Disciples of Christ Historical Society. Abiding
appreciation is expressed to these sources who funded the writing and publication
of this volume. These gifts have made it possible for many generations of Disciples
to know A. Dale Fiers, his faith, and the far reach of his ministry.

"What Duane Cummins has crafted here is a brief history of how a significant religious body dealt with the ambivalences of its own existence, how 'missionary work' developed into less paternalistic relationships, how a church struggled between its attempts to minister on the local scene and still recognize that the body of Christ is worldwide— and how one modest man could play a major role in all of that."

—ROBERT L. FRIEDLY, EDITOR EMERITUS, *THE DISCIPLE*

"D. Duane Cummins brings to this work his high standards for truth and clarity of expression as a skilled historian. He also communicates his high esteem for his subject, A. Dale Fiers. Readers have much to learn from this book on the pivotal years of twentieth-century Disciples history, those years leading up to restructure through the early years of its implementation. At the same time, readers are in for an often fascinating story of inspiration, integrity, and courage in the life of Dale Fiers, shepherd of the church through those transforming years."

—PETER M. MORGAN, PRESIDENT, DISCIPLES OF CHRIST HISTORICAL SOCIETY

"Duane Cummins has thoughtfully chronicled, in historic and caring detail, the story of the most significant leader of our church in the twentieth century. To have ministered by the side of A. Dale Fiers for a decade, at the zenith of his career, was an unparalleled privilege. I urge a wide reading of this important book among our membership.

—HOWARD E. DENTLER, RETIRED DEPUTY GENERAL MINISTER AND PRESIDENT

"This is an important biography that sheds much light on an essential era in the development of the Christian Church (Disciples of Christ) as well as telling the inspiring story of one of our church's greatest leaders. Duane Cummins has once again distinguished himself as a seminal historian of the church, weaving together the details of a leader's life with the events that shaped him and the church he led. This is a 'must read' for anyone who aspires to offer informed leadership in any manifestation of the Christian Church (Disciples of Christ)."

—RICHARD L. HAMM, GENERAL MINISTER AND PRESIDENT, CHRISTIAN CHURCH (DISCIPLES OF CHRIST)

To Betty

E LIZABETH C HUTE K UNZ
1909-1998

CONTENTS

❖　❖　❖　❖　❖　❖　❖　**ACKNOWLEDGEMENTS**

Dr. Peter Morgan, president of the Disciples of Christ Historical Society, proposed in early 1999 that I write a biography of A. Dale Fiers under the sponsorship of the historical society. I will be forever grateful to him for this suggestion. The research and writing of this volume became a labor of love, deepening my admiration and respect for Dale Fiers and for the generation of leaders who guided the church through restructure. In addition, my own understanding of those critical years has been deeply enriched.

The historical society acquired generous funding from the Oreon E. Scott Foundation to underwrite the cost of three years of research and through the philanthropy of Alan Fiers arranged for publication of the book by TCU Press. In addition, the historical society opened its extensive archives of Fiers material for my use. The staff archivists—David McWhirter and Sara Harwell, along with library staff Clint Holloway, Lynne Morgan, and Elaine Philpott —were helpful in countless ways, instructive, patient, and encouraging. They were always available to me and always helpful. To all of them I express sincere appreciation.

My most profound gratitude is extended to A. Dale Fiers who sat patiently for what must have seemed to him endless interviews and telephone conversations between 1999 and 2003. He was unfailingly gracious, sharing openly from the fullness of his personal files, his voluminous scrapbooks, seminary writings, photo albums and correspondence, and sharing candidly from both his heart and mind. He read each chapter in draft form, courteously informing me of an improper date, name, sequence of events, or fact whenever such appeared. Working with him was the single most rewarding writing and research experience

I have undertaken during my forty-six-year career. He was truly an inspiration.

I also express a deep indebtedness for advice, favors, and genuine helpfulness to Judith Furia, curator at the Kankakee County Historical Society, who uncovered city directories, histories, and photographs for my use; to Detra J. MacDougall at the Yale Divinity School Library who researched the Fiers academic records and copied the old catalogues for careful review; to R. Jeanne Cobb, archivist at the Bethany Archives, Bethany College, who generously assisted in researching the large Fiers collection of photographs, correspondence, and documents; to June Koelker and Bob Seal, librarians at TCU, for their kind assistance in acquiring materials through interlibrary loan; to Lawrence S. Steinmetz, yearbook editor for the Christian Church (Disciples of Christ), who thoughtfully provided old yearbook statistics; to Kenneth L. Teegarden, who so readily and graciously agreed to an extended interview on the leadership of A. Dale Fiers during restructure; to Alan Fiers who gener- ously shared his time for interviews, shared photographs, stories, and quite valuable letters; to Wayne Temple, deputy director of the Illinois State Archives; to the staff at the Indiana State Archives, who located the Fiers Civil War records; to Houston Bowers, who provided very helpful church papers, documents, and yearbooks from Euclid Avenue Christian Church in Cleveland; to Lois A. Hill, secretary at the Christian Church in Hamilton, Ohio, who provided vintage church publications and board minutes; to the gracious staff at Central Christian Church, Newark, Ohio, who generously provided old bulletins, papers, and other documents; to the church staff at Shadyside Christian Church, Shadyside, Ohio, who provided board minutes and other valuable information; to Dorothy "Dot" Howett, who gave helpful commentary on the interim ministry at First Christian Church in Miami, Florida; to Winnie Dillon and Carol Chambers, who shared insights about the interim ministry at Parkway

Christian Church; to Debi Murray, director of the Historical Society of West Palm Beach County, Florida, for graciously providing a large quantity of historical information on West Palm Beach; to Pat Mlodizk, who skillfully and patiently typed multiple drafts of the manuscript; to Teresa Palmer for her gracious and competent daily help in copying, collating, mailing, and distributing portions of the manuscript to various readers; and to Judy Alter, director of the TCU Press and her fine editorial staff, who gave the manuscript its final review.

I am deeply grateful to a group of scholars and friends—Lester McAllister, Howard Dentler, Robert Friedly, Mark Toulouse, Peter Morgan, Larry Steinmetz, Larry Grimes, Richard Hamm, and Robert Sandercox—who read the manuscript prior to its publication and graciously offered valuable advice, helping me to avoid historical and grammatical error. Any errors in the book, however, are exclusively my own.

Finally, and most importantly, I express my heartfelt appreciation to my wife, Suzi, for her sustained interest in and support of this work. Without her companionship, convivial spirit, and good cheer this volume could not have been written.

D. DUANE CUMMINS
JANUARY 1, 2003

Dale Fiers' niche in the history of the Disciples is a big one and it is secure! So is his place in our affections. Restructure towers over the landscape of modern Disciples history like a great mountain range, and A. Dale Fiers looms over the era as its central figure.

Our church learned from Dale that structure is far more an expression of an ideal than it is a practical concern for economy. He taught us that structure is an expression of church, a means to unity, a way to participate in the totality of church, a channel to ecumenical oneness. This contribution was crucial to the life and history of Disciples, and it will forever remain his compelling legacy to Discipledom and beyond.

Dale's distinguished presidency of the United Christian Missionary Society, his decisive role in restructure, and his influential leadership as the first general minister and president defined the office and guided the multitude of agencies through the implementation of the design until the new church settled and could function in an orderly way. Consequently, there is an enduring and powerful identity with Dale Fiers as the moving spirit behind restructure, a seminal moment in our modern history that many believe would not have been possible without him. It required a leader with spiritual force and the deep respect of the people to be able to stand against one of the most cherished traditions of our movement and say to us, "the local congregation is not the fullest expression of church." Others who knew less about "church" than Dale could not comprehend the awesome dimensions of its meaning—but Dale understood. His rich ministry had elevated his vision, enabling him to see possibilities and dream dreams for the thousands of scattered and disconnected

Disciples congregations. In his vision, they were an expression of church, not a law unto themselves.

When he was installed as executive secretary of the International Convention, he was serving simultaneously as president of the UCMS, executive secretary of the International Convention, and administrative secretary of the Commission on Restructure. Holding these three offices placed him in the compelling position of diplomatically prodding the commission processes to *develop* the proposal, judiciously guiding the convention processes to *approve* the proposal, and wisely shaping a smooth transition from the UCMS in order to *implement* the proposal. Dale's balanced and thoughtful statesmanship in these positions was absolutely essential to the success of restructure. His great legacy, believed Kenneth L. Teegarden, was helping the church find and grow into its new design.

It has been my intention to convey the journey of Dale's life of ministry, to identify the sources of moral and spiritual strength that empowered his life, and to record for future generations his soaring achievements for the Christian Church (Disciples of Christ). As much as possible I have tried to tell the story by letting Dale speak for himself, to base the narrative largely on his own words. The story contains glimpses of his inner journey, as well as the remarkable evolution of his public ministry rooted in the changing national environments that called forth his leadership.

Writing biography is a process of total immersion in the life of the subject. After reading the letters, studying the documents, conducting countless interviews with Dale, his friends, colleagues and relatives, I developed an ever-deepening respect and admiration for him, which I feel obliged to share with the reader at the outset. I believe Dale Fiers is truly a major figure in the history of the Christian Church (Disciples of Christ) and was undoubtedly its most important leader in the twentieth century.

D. DUANE CUMMINS
JANUARY 1, 2003

The Fiers 1740–1906

Ancestry and Heritage

Alan Dale Fiers was born December 17, 1906, in the rural, county seat town of Kankakee, Illinois. His boyhood and adolescence were lived in another small, county seat town. The Ohio county seat town congregations in Shadyside, Hamilton, and Newark provided the setting for his early ministry. The religious movement he would one day guide through restructure and help grow into a new expression of "church" was strategically plotted and planned on an early nineteenth century county seat town grid. The distinctive ethos of the small town, a sanctuary of hard work and simple values, shaped the contours of Dale's character as well as the character of the Disciples he would serve through a long and distinguished ministry. Among the hallmarks of these little towns are humanity and simplicity—hallmarks once described by Albert Camus as the only two things that really count in life.[1] Those hallmarks coupled with the folkways of the country town were infused into generations of Fiers, molding a family heritage defined by a rock-solid work ethic, a practical intelligence, an iron will, a resilient spirit, and an unflinching integrity—all leavened with an abiding human compassion—strands of character that would form a fundamental moral and spiritual core in the heart of A. Dale Fiers.

Kankakee County is about fifty miles south of Chicago. Without its two northwest townships, the county is a perfect rectangle extending thirty-eight miles east and west and twenty-one miles north and south. Its 679 square miles abut the state line of Indiana. Angling from the northeast out of the Indiana marshes is the quiet flow of the Kankakee River, pride of the prairie Potawatomi, whose great spirit once brooded over its waters. From the northwest flows the more hurried River Iroquois. The two rivers lie across the county like a chevron. Near their point of confluence is the county seat town of Kankakee, the heart of the Kankakee River Valley.[2] Like that of so many other counties, the proud history of Kankakee was fashioned by competing streams of immigration, Southerners preferring county government, Northeasterners preferring town government, and a dash of Canadians who gave the Kankakee River country a sprinkling of French. Here immigrant families, including the Fiers and Grubbs, blended their traditions into a unique community, distinct from those contributing to it and modified by the frontier experience. Kankakee would fight hard for its railroads and highways, for protection under the law, and for schools. From these struggles the county grew steadily if unspectacularly, forming a cast of mind marked by determination and perseverance.

The families of Dale's parents were not glaringly different. Primarily pioneer farmers and members of the small merchant class, they worked their way westward with the ever-moving line of the frontier. Not distinguished by high office or education, they were always among the first called upon to give their fathers, sons, and husbands to fight the nation's wars. Often their provincial environment was limiting and, on the surface of things, they may have seemed unlikely ancestors of an eminent church leader. Provincial communities hold their dangers, "insularity; regression into primitivism; complacence in the comforting familiarity of local scenes," as noted by Kenneth Clark. But he added, the most creative among provincial folk have "the vigor of fresh energies; they are immersed in and stimulated by the ordinary reality around them; and they transcend their limited environments by the sheer intensity of their vision, which becomes, at the height of their powers, prophetic."[3]

The ancestral road to Kankakee crossed two hundred years, five generations, and half a continent. It was the road that connected Dale to history, determined how he fit into society, shaped the features of his character, and informed him of why he was who he was. Dale's line of descent is direct from William Fiers, born in Sussex County, Virginia about 1740, the earliest known Fiers in America. From available evidence it seems likely the Fiers migrated from Holland and Belgium to Virginia during the early 1700s. A few descendants claim the family came from England while others favor a Flemish origin. William was married to Lucy Lawrence in 1760, and together they raised five children. He died in Southampton County, Virginia in 1815.[4] Little more is known of this early William Fiers, beyond the fact that he spent his life in southeast Virginia during the tumultuous days of the American Revolution and the presidencies from George Washington to James Madison. His eldest son, William, saw action in the Revolutionary War and claimed to have been present at Yorktown when the British surrendered.

Dale's lineage is traced to John Fiers, the second son of William and Lucy. John was born in Sussex County, Virginia, in 1762. Some twenty years later when his parents and siblings trekked southeastward to Southampton, John remained in Sussex and was listed on the tax roles as head of a household of three—himself, his wife Frances, and their daughter Sarah.[5] He and Frances would soon have six more offspring, and one can suppose the narrowness of his circumstances prompted the 1805 move westward to the new and promising two-year-old state of Ohio.

John was the first of his lineage to break away from the original seaboard states, journeying hundreds of miles into the Ohio Appalachian Plateau to establish a new home for his family. They probably traveled six or seven weeks in Conestoga wagons, carrying their household goods and tools through the Blue Ridge and the Appalachian mountains. Such a move over such a distance into a demanding environment was epic in scale. It required personal daring and more than a small amount of hard-nosed Hollander determination. Ohio, in 1805, was still heavily populated by Indians, including the Shawnee, Ottawa, Miami, Delaware, and Wyandot. It had been scarcely more than a decade since the famous battle of Fallen Timbers, near present-day Toledo, and it would be six more years before General Harrison's encounter with the Shawnee medicine man, The Prophet, at Tippecanoe in adjacent Indiana Territory. But John Fiers' decision was firm as granite, and the family settled in Greene County near the community of Xenia. There he farmed for several years, and it is believed practiced the trade of a cooper (barrel maker).

The sixth and next to youngest child of John and Frances was Thomas Lawrence Fiers, born August 30, 1798, the great-grandfather of Dale. Only seven when his family made its westward journey, he undoubtedly saw the experience through a young boy's eye as a thrilling adventure. By January of 1822, Thomas, then a veteran of the War of 1812, was married to Ann Lewis, and to this union were born twelve children. The Ohio years found him plying his trade as a cooper. Like his father before him, Thomas was lured farther west by the prospect of better fortune in the state of Indiana. He initially settled in Delaware County during the early 1840s. At that time, Indiana had only three cities of more than 2,500 people—Madison, New Albany, and Indianapolis—and the lines between rural and town life were vaguely formed. A decade later, Thomas moved his family on to Jay County, where they remained throughout the Civil War. Thomas died there about 1870. His government grave marker in the old pioneer cemetery in Redkey, Jay County, Indiana, reads simply: "Thomas L. Fiers - US Soldier - War of 1812."[6]

Lewis Fiers, son of Thomas and grandfather of Dale, was born in Xenia, Ohio, May 3, 1836, the ninth of twelve children. While still a small boy, he accompanied his family on its overland trek from Ohio to Indiana. Strength of will to face a test of courage was a recurring trait in the Fiers' lineage, and Lewis inherited it. Along with many of his Delaware County friends, Lewis responded to the formation of Company K of the 19th Regiment of Indiana volunteers on July 29, 1861, in Indianapolis. His younger brother, James, enlisted the same day. The 19th was part of the famous Iron Brigade, which, by war's end, led all other Union brigades in battlefield deaths. Assigned to the Army of the Potomac, Lewis saw action in many engagements, including Second Bull Run where his regiment held against the attack of Stonewall Jackson. He also participated in the battle of Antietam, the bloodiest encounter of the entire war, where the 19th entered with two hundred soldiers and emerged with thirty-seven. His brother James died of disease while serving in Company K. Lewis was discharged November 1, 1862, with disability following the battle of Antietam. Shortly after the war, he married Mary Frazier, and by 1868 was living in Iroquois County, Illinois, in the little village of Concord, just over the Indiana line, practicing the family trade as a cooper.[7]

Grandmother Mary (Frazier) Fiers was no shrinking violet when there was a clear call for courage or social conscience. She was remembered as an active member of the Women's Christian Temperance Union, uniform and all, whose idol was Carrie Nation. The family story is told of several barrels of liquor being destroyed in a speakeasy near Iroquois. The hounds traced the scent right to her front door. Standing in the doorway, feet planted firmly, hands on her hips, Grandmother Fiers said to the officers simply and forcefully, "Well!" There was no further investigation, no charge, no arrest.

Dale's father, George Alan Fiers, was born September 20, 1874, in Iroquois County, Illinois, the third of Lewis and Mary's four children. He was a self-made man with an extraordinary work ethic and an unfailing sense of humor, although there were times when he was given to moods of melancholy as if he carried the weight of the world on his shoulders. George was of modest stature, standing 5'7". He was known as a devout churchman, a great square dancer, and an excellent carpenter whose innate trustworthiness led his friends to describe him as "straight as a die." His grandson recalled, "George was a real charmer with a magnetic personality. Everybody liked to be around him when he was on key. He was always the life of the party."[8] During the years prior to his marriage, while living in Iroquois, he worked as a section hand on the Kankakee & Seneca Railroad for eighty-eight cents per day.[9] To supplement his income, George also worked part time as a hired hand on a farm near Iroquois—where he met his future wife, Leah Honor Grubbs.

❖   ❖   ❖   ❖   ❖

The ancestral line of Dale's mother, Leah Honor Grubbs, is first documented in Dearborn County, Indiana, where Otha Grubbs was born in 1818. His formative years on this primitive frontier are shrouded in obscurity. Even less is known about his wife whose last name was Allen. She was born in Virginia and later moved to Indiana as a small girl. There in Dearborn County, the couple met, married, and in 1855 produced a child, Edward Junior Grubbs, Dale's maternal grandfather. Although the Grubbs were living just four counties south of the Fiers, there is no record of the families being acquainted. Early in 1870, Otha Grubbs followed the time-honored tradition of moving his family westward to Iroquois, Illinois.[10] This was barely two years after Lewis Fiers had migrated to the same community. On December 30, 1875, Dale's grandfather, Edward Junior Grubbs, was married to Jessie Frances Graham in Iroquois, Illinois, at the parsonage of the Methodist minister.

Jessie's mother was the inimitable Leah Elizabeth Conway, a lyrical soul with a talent for acting who chose the life of the stage and during the Civil War years became widely known as the "Memphis Favorite." The Conway family disowned her because she had stepped outside the approved roles for women in the nineteenth century, and she never saw them again. On one of her many riverboat excursions, she met and married Frank Graham, a mercurial figure who became her business manager. While on his way to set a performance date for Leah, he fell overboard from a riverboat and drowned somewhere in the Mississippi in the early 1860s.[11] A daughter, Maggie, was their firstborn, followed in 1860 by their younger daughter, Jessie (Dale's grandmother), born in New Albany, Indiana. Leah's years on the meandering network of southern rivers were filled with danger and unexpected adventure. In the late fifties, the boat on which she was performing caught fire and sank. But the strong-willed Leah held on to her daughter, Maggie, and clung to a plank in the river for forty-eight hours before being rescued. Leah died some years later on an ocean voyage and much to the certain satisfaction of her free spirit she was buried at sea.[12]

Edward Junior Grubbs and his bride, Jessie Graham, planted their roots on an Illinois farm where they lived a more sedate and conventional life raising a family of ten children. Their eldest child, Leah Honor Grubbs, would become the mother of Dale Fiers. She inherited both the name and the resilient spirit of her legendary grandmother and became a compelling influence on her sisters, her parents, her husband, and particularly upon her son. She possessed a lively mind and an appreciation for literature and learning combined with common sense and a compassion for ministry. Decades later Leah's birth was lovingly recalled by her mother, Jessie. "Sixty years ago on the prairie of Illinois, near the town of Sheldon on the ninth of January, 1877 [Leah] was born. A bright child, she grew to be a splendid woman, a dutiful daughter, a gentle and helpful sister, a faithful, kind, and loving mother, and a true Christian."[13]

Leah's father was an ardent member of a Disciples congregation in Sciotaville. Among her lasting childhood impressions was her mother's baptism. "My earliest recollection of the church goes back to the same year in which I started to school in Sciotaville, Ohio—a little white meeting hall only two or three blocks from the Ohio River. There is just one incident I can remember out of that faraway time. There was a revival, and one moonlight night after the service we all went down to the river and I saw my mother walk out into the water where she was . . . baptized. I remember nothing of what was said or done in that little church, but I do know it put something into the heart of my father and mother that gave me a Christian home."[14]

Her girlhood years were spent in Iroquois, Illinois, where it was necessary for Leah to work to help support the growing number of Grubbs children. The moment she completed the eighth grade, the full extent of education Iroquois offered its population of 427, she was employed to teach all grades in the school. She also accepted part-time work with a neighboring farm family, assisting with household duties and farm chores. While working on this farm, the nineteen-year-old Leah met and fell in love with the blond-haired, wide-smiling hired hand, George Fiers, whom she quickly recognized as a good and principled man. They were married December 30, 1896. She later mused, "I never dreamed we would walk together through life."[15]

Her adolescent years generated in Leah a consuming interest in the church. Ministry, an unconventional role for women, became her dream, a dream accompanied with the hope of attending Eureka College. Family responsibilities and later her marriage combined to make it impossible for her to fulfill the Eureka hope. Like her grandmother before, Leah would not be turned from her dream. Eureka aside, she made arrangements to study under the tutelage of a well-known minister in Kent, Indiana. At frequent intervals, she traveled by horse and buggy from Iroquois to Kent, a distance of about twenty miles, where she pursued an intensive study of the Bible and the work of ministry with a man known simply as Pastor Crank. Although lacking a formal education for ministry, she acquired a remarkable knowledge of the Bible.

Tradition holds that Leah's ordination for ministry, a ceremony then conducted by local pastors and congregations, occurred in 1895, possibly at the Christian Church in Iroquois, where she had first made her

George and Leah Fiers, November 6, 1923

confession of faith and where she maintained her membership. That little congregation ceased to exist in the early part of the twentieth century, and its records were not preserved. For a brief time thereafter, she served local congregations in Illinois and Indiana as preacher and pastor. She always spoke warmly of Antioch Christian Church near Morocco, Indiana—"a beautiful white frame church with a tall steeple that stood in a little grove of oak trees by a brook"—where she was minister for more than a year.[16] Leah was a determined pioneer for women in ministry and one of the earliest in the history of the Disciples to receive the distinction of ordination.

Birth of a New Child, a New Century, a New Church

In 1906, the year of Dale Fiers' birth, the progressive Theodore Roosevelt was in the fifth year of his presidency. Thousands were still living who had served with Robert E. Lee and Ulysses S. Grant, but the old order was passing and a new age was making a dramatic debut with the automobile, the airplane, and the motion picture. By this year, America had advanced to the status of a world power and could look back over three generations of unparalleled material progress including the settlement of a continent.[17] The population, enjoying religious freedom and free public education, had reached approximately seventy-eight million and boasted one of the highest standards of living anyplace in the world. "T. R." believed his country had earned the right to carry a big stick in advocacy of its ideals.

But the growth of wealth was generating certain problems for the democracy. By 1906, the Industrial Revolution, the rise of the city, the growth of big business, the redistribution of wealth, racism, child labor, political corruption, and a steady growth of immigration had combined to create ethical confusion throughout the society. A political reform movement known as Progressivism rejected the concept of laissez-faire strategies, calling instead for a strong central government to regulate industry, finance, transportation, agriculture, labor, and even morals. Rooted in a Protestant ethic, Progressive thought included great concern for the poor, the underprivileged, women, children, immigrants, and blacks. The government, more so than the church, offered the most profound response to the social challenges of the day.

In retrospect, there are those who suggest that faith in God had faded against the backdrop of the emerging modern age. Scholars believe the Victorian era had suffered a crisis of faith. The nineteenth century mind had been forced to choose between faith and reason, between giving up intellectual honesty or abandoning the religious and spiritual dimension of life. Religion as a cohesive social force had begun to weaken.[18] By some accounts, Europe was beginning to discard Christianity altogether. Near the time of Dale Fiers' birth, the English poet, Thomas Hardy, wrote a poem symbolizing the time in which he imagined himself attending "God's funeral."[19]

However, the late nineteenth century was also a time of peace movements, temperance movements, crusades, and the social gospel. But it would be the mid-twentieth century before the church would unveil the concept of liberation theology, a concept birthed by a younger generation of preachers and leaders educated in sociological concerns, social issues, and social action and who were seeking a response to the social ills of the new industrialization. The eighteenth century had reduced mystery to reason, according to Jaroslav Pelikan, and flattened transcendence into common sense. Nineteenth-century romanticism, in his judgment, then rose as a protest against the old orthodoxies.[20] The new twentieth-century concept of liberation theology would introduce the use of Jesus' prophetic opposition to the economic and social injustice of his time as the dynamic for revolutionary change in the ordering of human relations both public and private. Jesus was presented as one who challenged every social system and called it into account before the judgment of God, while the Epistle of Paul to the Galatians would be read in this new century as the Magna Carta of Christian liberty.

The year Dale Fiers was born, the so-called Disciples Brotherhood, a synonym for the forbidden word "denomination," was nearly seventy-five years old and planning to celebrate the centennial of the Declaration and Address three years later in Pittsburgh. The modern democracy of big business, big labor, and big cities had long since outgrown the social views and simple frontier formulas of the church fathers. The church was now surrounded by the extremes of poverty and wealth, and it struggled with its responsibility for ministering amidst the social and intellectual turmoil of the modern age. It struggled, too, with the application of scientific disciplines to the scriptures and the changing views of biblical interpretation they produced. And, of course, its greatest struggle was with the very nature of religious authority and how to structure its polity for effective mission.[21] These struggles would shape the history of the Disciples in the twentieth century. In fact, in the year of Dale Fiers' birth, 1906, a statistical division occurred within the Disciples when 430,000 members of the 1,120,000-member movement affirmed their separate identity as Churches of Christ (a cappella). This separation grew directly out of the tension-filled maze of biblical interpretation, church structure and authority, and the nature of ministry in the new social environment. One side held to the older, less complicated way and closed its doors and its mind to the new age. The other side of the movement attempted to come to terms with the advancing social and intellectual developments of the country. These different responses to the modernization of late-nineteenth-century American culture help explain the controversies that beset Disciples at the moment of Dale Fiers' birth.

By 1906, George and Leah Fiers had a family of two daughters, Othel and Bethel. Leah's ministry and George's work with the railroad supplemented by farm jobs and carpentry provided their livelihood. George sought a better life for his family and decided to risk the full-time occupation of carpentry and building. In 1904 he moved his family to Kankakee, where he constructed two bungalows on Sibly Street, selling one and moving into the other. Their son Alan Dale Fiers was born in the second bungalow, during the early chill of winter, December 17, 1906, as one year was ending and another about to begin—a birth poised in time between the ending of a frontier past and the beginning of an unsettling new age for both the culture and the church.

CHAPTER TWO

Childhood to Marriage 1906–1931

Early Childhood Days in Kankakee

In 1906, Kankakee, with a population exceeding thirteen thousand, was enjoying the final years of small-town supremacy in America. Similar to other American towns, Kankakee, a nineteenth-century creation, was northern enough to be industrial, southern enough to have a rural aspect, eastern enough to have a past, and western enough to have once been on the frontier. Like most of America at that time, it was still a horse-drawn community. Three years after Dale's birth, William Howard Taft rode to his inauguration in a horse and carriage, the last president to do so. Photographs of Kankakee taken during the first decade of the twentieth century show horse-drawn carriages, buggies, and wagons parked along its streets. Even the Kankakee fire wagon was still propelled by a team of horses. But tracks for the electric trolley were clearly visible in the center of those same streets, a harbinger of the approaching age.[1]

The sounds of trains in the night were among Dale's earliest memories of Kankakee—engines on the big four railroad lines sounding their whistles as they pulled into the station at the end of Merchant Street. On that same street was Whitmore's Grocery where George Fiers paid the family grocery bill every Saturday. The memory was a vivid one for Dale because Mr. Whitmore always gave him a sack of chocolates when he

Kankakee, 1906: Corner of Merchant and Schuyler, looking toward the railroad station

accompanied his father to pay the bill. Nearby on Court Street was the ice cream parlor where Dale happily consumed his first chocolate ice cream soda. Down the way at 237 Schuyler was a barber-and-billiard shop, with six chairs in front and a room in back containing ten billiard tables owned and operated by Lewis Fiers, Dale's uncle, known to him simply as Uncle "Cad." Dale's father once took him to that billiard room for a telegraphed broadcast of the Jess Williard and Jack Johnson heavy-weight title fight. The smoke in the room was so intense that young Dale lost consciousness and had to be taken outside to revive.[2]

During those pre–World War I days, the family enjoyed a solid level of prosperity in Kankakee. George's domain was the construction site. He was a general contractor who built houses, lived in some of them briefly, and then sold them for a good profit. The family, across the years of

Dale's infancy and early childhood, lived variously at 240 Sibley Street, 82 River Street, 39 Poplar Avenue, and 360 South Schuyler, just one block from Uncle Cad's barber-and-billiard shop.[3] They always had electricity but never a telephone, although telephones had been in Kankakee since 1903. George Fiers was one of the first in town, however, to own an automobile. By 1909, only sixty-two persons in the whole of Kankakee owned a horseless carriage. George, who often took his family to the fairgrounds to see displays of these new machines, purchased a Hupmobile, an auto first manufactured in 1909.[4] The two-toned red-and-black car with its acetylene lamps for headlights, four-cylinder engine, and two-speed transmission was the pride of George Fiers. When Dale's mother, Leah, drove it for the first time, she ran into a horse-drawn milk wagon, an incident abruptly ending her driving career. Dale recalled several thirty-mile trips to Iroquois to visit Grandmother Fiers, with his father sitting proudly at the wheel.

Another of his enduring Kankakee memories was Gougar's Grove. Captain Billy Gougar hauled passengers up and down the Kankakee River on his excursion boats the *Margarit* and the *Minnie Lillie*. Near a grove of trees that bore Gougar's name were several picnic tables and a refreshment house. The Fiers and Grubbs families often visited the grove, sometimes camping overnight with their close friends the Klaisses or with Uncle Cad and Aunt Bessie. Dale remembered his Uncle Burgess Grubbs once swimming across the Kankakee River at Gougar's Grove and thought at the time it was tantamount to swimming the English Channel. When he later visited the site as an adult, Dale discovered he could spit nearly across the river at that point.[5]

The greatest adventure of Dale's preschool years in Kankakee was a train trip to Florida during the winter of 1910–1911. George had become aware that Florida was poised for a building boom and decided to make an exploratory trip with his family, including Grandmother Fiers, to determine if such a move was worth the risk. George and Leah purchased a pair of goggles for four-year old Dale to wear so he could peer out the train windows without getting coal dust and cinders in his eyes. He remembers his mother awakening him in the night to show him and his sisters the Ohio River near Sciotaville where as a little girl she had lived near the river's edge.

The trip progressed into the Deep South and into the depths of new cultural mores. Leah's initiation to Jim Crow laws and the widespread mistreatment of minorities became one of the family's cherished stories. "We pulled into a Florida train station," Dale recalled, "and Mother looked out the window to see the name of the town. 'We are in Colo— Red,' she announced. Then she saw the word "White" over another entrance door of the station, and the penny dropped. It was our first contact with segregated facilities." Racial attitudes were not closely scrutinized in those days, and few complained about such insulting practices. Five decades later Dale would play an important national role helping to remove the ugly stain of racism.

Following their arrival in West Palm Beach, George, in an orderly and businesslike manner, explored other areas of the state. First, he visited Tampa where he bought ten acres of land and held it until 1925, when it was lost in the Florida bank runs and the depression. Later the family assessed the Miami area where they attended the First Christian Church, for which Dale would serve as interim seventy years later. Ultimately they returned to the Palm Beach area where they were most satisfied. Here the Fiers glimpsed their future, and George, during their return trip to Illinois, began thinking through preparations for the relocation.

Dale began first grade at Kankakee's Von Steuben School in 1912, the year Woodrow Wilson was elected president. The school was nearby, and Dale walked the distance each day, usually stopping at the candy store on his way home to buy a one-cent piece of chocolate. At first he sat on the back row in a class of twenty-five to thirty students. When the teacher noticed that he was not responding verbally to her questions, she moved him to the front row, which helped address his shyness. Overcoming the shyness would require many years. During his high school years a decade later, Dale recalled even then the "absolute torture" of verbal recitations in his English class.

Every Sunday and religious holiday the Fiers family unfailingly attended the Christian Church. Leah taught in the church school, led Bible studies, and occasionally preached. George remodeled the church in 1908–1909. Aside from the county fair, the church socials provided most of the socialization for the family. The church and the family set moral standards as they did in most country towns. Yet in spite of their many virtues, these little towns were capable of imposing conformity and a morality so rigid it could suffocate a creative spirit. Not so with the Fiers in either Kankakee or later. Their religion was real, authentic, and integral to their lives, but it was not worn on their sleeves. Mealtime prayer was irregular, and there were no Bible readings or Bible study in the home. But Dale was taught to kneel by his bedside each night to pray, and there was a naturalness in talking about God or having occasional religious discussions around the table at mealtime. In later years, the family read *The Lookout* and *The Christian Standard*. They also read from their mother's library in their home, a library affectionately called "Mother's missionary things." Dale's mental world was suffused with a heavy religious orientation. The church was clearly the center of their social and moral life. Mother Leah enforced a moral discipline born of conservative Disciples tradition which included no card playing, no dancing, and later no movies or sports on Sundays. But it was not a stifling, fundamentalist environment designed to control or exclude. It was a religious household that respected a healthy blend of religious thought and individual spiritual freedom tempered with religious tradition.[6]

By 1913, George had completed building the houses he had contracted in Kankakee, sold his business, his home, and his Hupmobile.
Along with Leah's parents, her six brothers and their families, the Fiers
entourage moved to Florida, settling in West Palm Beach, the setting for
Dale's late boyhood and adolescence.[7]

Boyhood Years in West Palm Beach

Historians record that on January 9, 1878, the *Providencia*, carrying a
cargo of coconuts from Trinidad, sank near Palm Beach. Residents
quickly salvaged and planted the cargo. The many new trees consequently inspired the name of their settlement. In 1887, President
Grover Cleveland appointed a postmaster for Palm City. When it was
discovered a place of that name already existed, it was changed to West
Palm Beach.[8]

By 1893, the pioneer period in the region had ended. The first school
was founded in 1886; the *Indian River News* was established in 1897; and
the Lake Worth Railroad opened in 1890. Between 1885 and 1913, the
year of the Fiers' arrival, the person most responsible for the development
of this coastal area was Henry Morrison Flagler. He built railroads, plotted the city of West Palm Beach, and constructed a number of luxury
hotels including the Cordova, the Alcazar, the Royal Poinciana, and the
Breakers to which Dale, during his teenage years, would deliver papers.
Flagler created an island of affluence, ranked among the top five resorts
for the nation's wealthy.

In 1900, West Palm Beach had a population of 564; by 1910, shortly
before the Fiers arrived, it had reached 1,743,—8,659 by 1920, and thirty-
six thousand by 1930. George Fiers' decision to make the move was
surely a wise one. His general contractor skills were much in demand in
the booming environment of West Palm Beach. The county itself had a
population of approximately 5,500 (3,314 white and 2,220 black) in

The Little Brown Church in West Palm Beach: Dale and friends

1910, only one year after its incorporation. By 1920, its population had more than tripled to 18,654.[9]

Work was abundant when the Fiers and Grubbs arrived in 1913. Grandfather Grubbs and his six sons preferred large housing developments, building most of Palm Beach Heights, along with an entire row of houses on Chicago Street. George preferred individual contracts for single houses, hotels, or theaters. Following the practice begun in Kankakee, he built houses, lived in them briefly, and sold them for a profit. The family moved regularly, living variously on Sixth, Twelfth, Thirteenth, Poinsettia, Rockport, and Kings Court. Both families, each using a different business strategy, became financially successful. George, a member of the Modern Woodmen of America, built many homes in West Palm Beach and Lake Park; at one time he served as mayor of Lake Park.[10]

He was also an elder and charter member of the new Christian Church established at West Palm Beach in 1914. O. J. Bulfin and Leah Fiers were co-ministers, the former retired and the latter a volunteer. In its first year the little congregation reported a membership of sixteen to the yearbook. It met for a time in the Odd Fellows Hall on Dixie Highway but soon purchased a $1,500 lot on the corner of Lakeview and Olive streets. George drew up plans for "a little brown church," organized all the men of the congregation, and purchased the lumber and supplies. The Little Brown Church was virtually completed in a single day, with the men working the construction, women cooking and serving food, and the children doing cleanup and chores. "The building served as home for the growing congregation until 1925," wrote Dale, "when the White Temple was built on Hibiscus Avenue to provide a more adequate facility. My father planned and supervised the construction of both buildings. My mother served as one of two volunteer ordained ministers in the early years of the congregation's life until resources were sufficient to employ a full-time pastor." In 1917, the congregation reported twenty participating members and was contributing $13.61 to missions ($3 for the American Christian Missionary Society, $6 for the Foreign Christian Missionary Society, and $4.61 for the National Benevolent Association).[11]

The very configuration of outreach giving from the Little Brown Church in West Palm Beach was a reflection of the uncoordinated structure of the Disciples church beyond the local congregation. Competition for these congregational dollars combined with theological principle again nudged cooperative Disciples toward a new ecclesiastical structure—a never-ending search. At the 1919 Cincinnati International Convention, a recommendation was approved to form a new cooperative venture named the United Christian Missionary Society, an agency A. Dale Fiers would one day serve as president longer than any other person.[12]

Critics were bountiful, developing their attacks upon the UCMS around the fear of ecclesiastical power and the fear of women in positions of authority. These issues were compounded by the "open membership" controversy (accepting unimmersed persons as members)—openly defended by few, quietly practiced by many—and the issue of intellectual control over the College of the Bible at Lexington, Kentucky. Dale would not have the opportunity to serve an "open membership" congregation until his interim assignments during retirement. The 1917 "heresy trial" in Lexington established historical critical study of Scriptures (as contrasted to a literal reading and acceptance of Scriptures) as the predominant intellectual force among Disciples throughout his future ministry.

The 1918 Medbury Resolution, demanding the Foreign Christian Missionary Society forbid unimmersed from joining churches in China, and the 1925 resolution in the Oklahoma City Convention to "recall any missionary who believed in acceptance of unimmersed into its church membership" were ultimately repudiated. But it launched a gradual withdrawal from fellowship of another large segment of the Campbell-Stone Movement known as the Christian Churches and Churches of Christ. Separation actually began at the 1926 International Convention in Memphis, Tennessee, with a rump convention held in the Pantages Theater, where the North American Christian Convention was first organized.[13] These national events, swirling beyond the little West Palm Beach congregation would impact and shape Dale's ministry in the years to come—events to which he was mostly oblivious as a teenager. He did, however, recall meeting missionaries who visited the small congregation. He especially remembered E. B. Quick, the regional director of Christian education for the UCMS.

His religious development in the church was supplemented with a variety of other experiences. Along with his whole family, he heard William Jennings Bryan speak at the First Congregational Church in West Palm Beach. They also attended the tent meetings of traveling evangelists, among them Jones and Reisner. Reisner built a temporary tabernacle in West Palm Beach, on the shores of Lake Worth, where he held services for three weeks. Dale joined the youth choir that sang at the services. One evening when Reisner invited persons to come forward, no one came. Then he asked members of the audience to kneel if there was something troubling them or they wanted to pray for someone. Nine-year-old Dale noticed his mother kneeling in the audience and thought she might be praying for him, so he walked forward. It was a deeply emotional experience for him. He went straight home, talking to no one, and went directly to bed on the sleeping porch. Later his mother came in, knelt by his bedside, and said a prayer.

Dale's confession of faith in the evangelist's tent was followed shortly by baptism in the fall of 1915. O. J. Bulfin baptized him along with ten girls in the local Baptist church because the Little Brown Church did not as yet have a baptistry. Soon after, his two older sisters asked if he would like to join the Tenth Legion. It sounded exciting to Dale, and he said yes. The Tenth Legion turned out to be a group of young people who had made a pledge to tithe. Although not quite the image of high adventure Dale had in mind, the Tenth Legion introduced the habit of tithing he has maintained for a lifetime.

Leah was unquestionably the strongest influence in Dale's young life. He spoke of her intense love of the Bible and the great respect she generated from all persons who knew her. When something was wrong in the Grubbs family the intuitive response was almost always, "Go get Aunt Lizzie," as she was known to them. She took pleasure and strength from her church and from her books. When she was emotionally moved, she would often write a poem or letter. Dale recalled her great sense of humor. He also recalled when she became upset with him, she expressed her displeasure in words while his father expressed his displeasure with a switch under the mango tree in the backyard. When asked when he volunteered his life for ministry, Dale responded, "I think I volunteered my life for ministry when I was still in my mother's womb." Actually he

Dale and his parents in West Palm Beach

made that decision in junior high, a decision prompted by his friends at church and by his mother.

West Palm Beach gave Dale a small-town childhood where, apart from church and school activities, children made their own diversions. For a time he lived in a house known as Park Cottage on the shore of Lake Worth, where he enjoyed fishing off the dock at the end of the street and swimming in the ocean. He also enjoyed attending outdoor five-cent movies, camping with the Boy Scouts, observing the abundance of diamondback rattlesnakes in the town, gathering turtle eggs along the shore, listening to the Bockman Million Dollar Band playing concerts in the park, and going to Clematis Street on Saturday nights just to watch the people. Once his sister, Othel, dared him to ride his bicycle off the end of the city dock, promising two dollars if he did it. "Forthwith," remembered Dale, "I got on my bike and made a glorious splash off the dock into eight feet of water. I rescued my bike and collected the two dollars."

The bicycle was very important to him because he was the Palm Beach paperboy. "I delivered papers for the *Palm Beach Post*," he recalled.

"Later I had a *Palm Beach Times* route, and for another period I delivered the *Miami Herald*. At one time, I delivered the *Post* to the entire town of Palm Beach, including the Royal Ponciana, the Bradley Club, and the old Breakers Hotel. During the season the route had to be divided due to the influx of tourists."[14]

DeWitt Brown was the circulation manager for the *Miami Herald*. He and Dale became good friends. When Dale took him home to meet the family, DeWitt promptly fell in love with Dale's sister, Othel, who possessed the free spirit of her father and was very close to Dale. DeWitt and Othel were soon married and entered the magazine and newspaper distribution business. In the 1980s they gave eight million dollars to the Disciples, at the time the largest unrestricted gift ever given to an American Protestant church.

Another of his favorite diversions was playing the banjo. He purchased his first banjo in 1922 for $125 saved from his paper route. It was a Washburn manufactured by Lyon and Healy out of Chicago. In 2002 he was still playing the same banjo, worth more than ten times what he paid for it in 1922. Still another diversion was taking a boat out Jupiter Inlet to fish, a somewhat risky business because the inlet had never been dredged. Using his crystal set, with its aerial extended out of the window, he often listened to ships sending Morse code on nearby waterways. As he grew older, Dale worked for his father during the summer months and became an apprentice in the Guild of Carpenters and Joiners, lacking only one more summer of work to become a journeyman.

Dale lived his early years in West Palm Beach under the cloud of World War I. In June of 1914, the year the new Christian church was established, Archduke Ferdinand was assassinated, a shot that determined the course of history for the twentieth century. In 1915, the year of Dale's baptism, the *Lusitania* was sunk. On Good Friday in 1917, the United States declared war, and in November, one month before Dale's eleventh birthday, the Russian Revolution spilled its blood upon the world. Wartime scenes were as close as the park near Dale's home during 1917 and 1918.

"When the war came the park was a staging area for the troops before they embarked for Europe. I would go watch them . . . and follow them to the railroad station to wave goodbye when the troops were sent on their way. . . . It was while we lived on Kings Court that the Armistice was declared, November 18, 1918. It was nighttime when the news came. Everyone in town, it seemed, rushed down Clematis Avenue to celebrate. I remember marching up and down the street as impromptu parades formed."[15]

He remembered, too, the cemetery across the street from their Kings Court home. The legacy of death on such a scale during the war years caused him to notice the words above the gate. "I was fascinated by the words in the wrought iron arch over the entrance to the cemetery— 'That which is so universal as death must be a blessing.' My mother and father are buried within its gates. The old arch is gone but the words are still there, now in stone. Each time I enter I ponder the far-reaching parameters of their meaning."[16]

In 1914, Dale began his second-grade year in the West Palm Beach school system. On his first day, a group of boys threw him to the ground and tore open his shirt to see if he was really a "blue-bellied Yankee." The school was located on "The Hill" at the west end of Hibiscus Street, a single building that housed all elementary and high school classes. Soon another building was added, and finally the new high school, making a first-class educational campus and arguably one of the best school systems in Florida at that time. Dale's class of 1925 was the first to graduate from the new school.

While the passage of time has taken a heavy toll on the physical condition of the campus, it still stimulated grand memories for Dale. "Who could ever forget a principal reading the thirteenth chapter of First Corinthians at every student assembly where he presided. Nor can the memory of a later principal, Ruby Lorence, be easily erased. Her impos- ing presence as she walked through study hall exuded authority. There was a superb faculty. Teachers like Emily Keyes made English exciting. Margaret Young guided us through Latin. Then there was Coach Henry Wood whose pre-game pep talks worked us into a frenzy just short of an intention to kill. . . . In ways known and unknown they left the stamp of their influence upon my life . . . time and circumstance have diminished and dispersed the company of friends and teammates that gave meaning to those Palm Beach High years. I still wander through the *Royal Palm* yearbooks and relive those days."[17] There was certainly a lot to relive, including a role in the cast of the senior play, *A Pair of Sixes*, the thrill of watching Babe Ruth play in a West Palm Beach exhibition game, but most especially the assistance of his English teacher, Emily Keyes, helping him control his fears and gain confidence in public speaking. He gradu- ated in 1925 with a B average, scoring his highest marks in chemistry, algebra, and English composition.[18]

The memories of his athletic prowess were exceptionally vivid. Dale, a three-sport letterman at West Palm Beach High, was voted the out- standing athlete in his graduating class and has since become a Florida legend, receiving many special recognitions including induction into the West Palm Beach Distinguished Alumni Hall of Fame. From 1923 through 1925 the sports pages of the *Palm Beach Post* regularly carried articles telling of "Casey" Fiers' feats of excellence as a fullback, punter, and kicker on the football squad and first baseman and fifth-place hitter on the baseball team. When the West Palm Beach football team played Daytona in 1924, the following day's headline read, "Fiers Stars for Palm Beach," and the body of the four-column article read in part: "The after- noon might appropriately be called 'Casey' Fiers' Day. He proved to be a

Dale's football team at West Palm Beach, fall, 1923. Dale is first on the left in the back row

tower of strength on the defense and must have seemed a demon on the offense to the opposition. He made the only touchdowns scored in the first half and kicked the point after touchdown on four occasions . . . Fiers circled right end for a long run of 32 yards . . . Fiers circled left end for an 18-yard run."[19]

Against Fort Pierce that year Dale scored two touchdowns, and the paper reported "Casey Fiers was the thorn in the side of the visitors . . . dashing around right end on a crisscross pattern four plays before the game ended for the last touchdown." Late in the season, the West Palm Wildcats played the St. Augustine Yellow Jackets, defeating them thirteen to nothing. Writing of Dale's performance, the sports columnist noted, "Fiers, star Palm Beach fullback, scintillated as usual, breaking up many St. Augustine plays and dodging and twisting through tacklers for long gains nearly every time he carried the ball."[20] During his senior year, Dale scored nine touchdowns, kicked twenty-two extra points, and was considered one of the finest high school football players in the state. His mother had opposed his playing football. One of Dale's great memories was running to make a tackle near the sidelines where his mother was seated and hearing her yell, "Get him, Dale! Get him." In his senior year, he was named to the position of fullback on the Florida All-State Team.

Baseball, however, was Dale's first love and the *Post* reported his extraordinary accomplishments on the diamond just as it had on the gridiron. After an early season game against Delray, won by West Palm, a typical account appeared in the next day's sports pages: "Casey Fiers was the big gun in the offense, crashing a homer to Sadler's sign in left center with the bases completely populated in the first inning . . . again in the fourth Casey stepped to the plate with three runners waiting to come in. Casey didn't disappoint them, this time with a double. He scored later and sent in another run in the sixth . . . driving in or scoring a total of eleven runs. Not a bad day's work for anyone in any league."[21] His greatest thrill came in an eighteen-inning game against Miami in 1924 to determine the southeast regional championship. West Palm Beach won the game by a score of six to four. The key hit of the game was Dale's triple in the first inning with the bases loaded.

Dale's hitting was so prolific it often overshadowed his outstanding defensive skill at first base. But one sportswriter took notice: "The third sacker . . . threw wild to first, but Casey Fiers reached out into nowhere and gathered the pellet in. Casey made another hair trigger stop in the seventh on the same kind of play." It was Dale's good fortune to play with a highly talented group of athletes who won multiple championships in several sports. Sportswriters of the day recognized the unusual ability of this West Palm Beach team calling it "the best team in years and probably the best team in its history." Dale's parents kept a scrapbook of their son's distinguished athletic accomplishments; the scrapbook had a little note on the cover, "Proud parents often serve history by preserving the records of a modest son."[22] Everyone who knew his father, George Fiers, said he loved nothing so much as watching his son play ball.

The year 1925 was a year of loss for George and Leah Fiers. Bethel had earlier married a bank teller in the same bank where she also worked as a teller. At Christmastime 1925, Othel, who was working at an architectural firm, married DeWitt Brown, the man introduced to her by her brother, Dale. In the fall of 1925, there was a run on the Florida banks following the peak of the land boom, and George was forced to withdraw his resources from Farmer's Bank and Trust. Residents, of course, could no longer afford to build and had less need to hire general contractors, causing the Grubbs family to leave West Palm Beach that same fall and resettle in St. Charles, Missouri. It was also the year word came of Grandmother Fiers' death in Iroquois, Illinois. Dale remembered when his father received the news he was working on the church. Since their move in 1913, they had returned to Iroquois on two occasions to visit Grandmother Fiers and on one visit had built a garage for her.

And of course 1925 was the year Dale left home to attend college. His sister, Othel, had been the first to go to college and did so against her father's wishes. But he paid for her to attend Piedmont Baptist College in Georgia for one year. Dale received considerable pressure from his friends to attend the University of Florida and continue his athletic career, but he wanted to be a minister. He considered Disciples schools—Texas Christian University and Drake University and also Butler University, where a school of religion was opening in the fall. J. H. Bristor, his West Palm Beach pastor, urged him to go to Bethany, the oldest of the Disciples colleges, which Bristor called the "fountainhead." So he decided to attend Bethany College in Bethany, West Virginia, even though some said he was setting his feet in Sodom because Bethany had an athletic cheer with the word "hell" in it. To pay the cost to attend Bethany, Dale and nine of his friends, all of whom worked at the *Palm Beach Post*, jointly purchased a $10,000 lot in Boca Raton for $1,000 down ($100 each). The profit from the sale of this property, they speculated, would finance their college education, but the land boom burst and by Christmas they had lost it all.

George Fiers would have preferred that Dale remain as his business partner in a firm he would name "Fiers and Son." But if Dale's wish was

Dale, age eighteen

to become a minister, George promised to help provide the best ministerial education available. Leah later told Dale that when he left on the
long train ride for college, George came home, laid his head on the table,
and wept.

The Education of a Bethany College Man

The trip to Bethany College, a campus Dale had never seen, required
two-and-one-half days. He rode the East Coast Railroad from West Palm
Beach to Jacksonville. From the old Jacksonville station he took the train
to Washington, DC. At Washington, he boarded the Pennsylvania Railroad
to Pittsburgh, where he connected with the Baltimore & Ohio to
Wheeling, West Virginia. From Wheeling, he again boarded the
Pennsylvania Railroad to Wellsburg, where he completed the trip to
Bethany on the Toonerville Trolley. Riding the trolley that day was a
Bethany student, Don Boyd, who also happened to be a member of
the Beta Theta Pi fraternity. When they reached Bethany, Don escorted
Dale directly to the Beta house, sealing his destiny in the Greek system.
Dale was both happy and privileged to be at Bethany. During the days of
Calvin Coolidge, only one in seven attended college and only one of two
attended high school.[23]

When Dale arrived in the fall of 1925, the eighty-five-year-old, pic-
turesque little campus with its dirt streets had only five buildings—
Cochran Hall, Carnegie Library, Irwin Gymnasium, Phillips Hall, and Old
Main. It was the year West Penn Power Company brought electricity to
the campus. The faculty numbered about twenty-nine, three of whom had
a Ph.D. Most of the remainder held masters degrees, predominantly from
Columbia University. Total enrollment hovered around 375. Nearly all of
the students came from small towns and rural areas within a hundred miles
of Bethany. They hailed from the hill-country towns of Pennsylvania and
West Virginia and from the river towns and farm communities of Ohio.

Dale's arrival at Bethany College in the fall of 1925

Dale, being from Florida, was clearly an anomaly. Of the 134 freshmen enrolled that September of 1925 only forty-two would graduate (thirty-two percent) with Dale in 1929. Along the way, thirteen transfers swelled the number in the class of 1929 to fifty-six. There was almost an even number of men and women among those who stayed the full four years—twenty-two men and twenty-one women. Eighty-six percent of the graduating class came from the tri-state area—fourteen from Pennsylvania, thirteen from Ohio, ten from West Virginia, two from Florida, two from New York, one from Connecticut, and one from Michigan. There were no international students and no ethnic minorities.[24]

In 1925, Disciples institutions still adhered to founder Alexander Campbell's educational philosophy, but with a stronger sectarian tone. Most of them, including Bethany, were best characterized as Bible colleges with significant numbers of students preparing for ministry in the Christian Church. The presidents of these colleges were, almost to a person, ordained Disciples ministers. General education requirements at Bethany included six hours of English, sixteen hours of science and math, fourteen hours of foreign language, twelve hours of history and social sciences, twelve hours of philosophy, religious education and education, six hours of Bible, and four hours of physical education.

The decade of the 1920s saw the philosophies of Alfred North Whitehead, William James, and John Dewey gain influence with curriculum builders. James believed one of the essential parts of a liberal education was to know the chief rival attitudes toward life. "A person with no philosophy," he wrote, "is the most inauspicious and unprofitable of all social mates."[25] Whitehead argued, "you may not divide the seamless coat of learning," and the subjects of "general education are special subjects specially studied."[26] Dewey in his *Democracy and Education: An Introduction to the Philosophy of Education* wrote that education and experience were synonymous and that education should not be segregated from society.

With World War I and later the depression changing the American experience, people sought a larger context for their specialized knowledge; they sought to integrate their experience with education. This impulse gave rise to the general education movement begun at Columbia University in 1919. Academia was also developing a deeper appreciation for economics, political science, sociology, and psychology—a body of courses known as the social sciences, designed to strengthen the relationship between education and society by providing, through scholarly study, a greater breadth of understanding of people and institutions.

The curriculum required of Dale at Bethany as a ministerial student was heavily oriented toward preparing him in his major. Greek, of course, counted as the foreign language requirement, but it was the intention of Bethany to offer ministerial students an education "equal in thoroughness and comprehensiveness to that offered in the best seminaries."[27]

Among the legendary Bethany professors who made a substantial impact upon him was Irvin Taylor Green in New Testament and homiletics. Professor Green once told Dale, "You cannot shortchange the country churches. These folk have their hand on the plow all week, and they have time to think about what you said in your sermon. In the city, they can't tell you the next day what you said." In reflection, Dale commented on his own sermons during his student minister years, "I have often thought I should refund money to those churches for the poor sermons I preached." Other professors whose contributions were written deep into his thinking included Henry Newton Miller in Christian education, Professor Gershon Samuel Bennett in Old Testament, Professor Frank Roy Gay in Greek, and Professor Andrew Leitch, chair of the newly created psychology department.

The last half of the 1920s was an uneasy period in which the world was attempting to adjust to the aftermath of World War I. Established landmarks of thought, values, and social order were changing. Dale experienced these changes. Although he and his family carefully followed the Scopes trial during the summer of 1925, he arrived at Bethany believing the earth was created in 4004 B.C., according to the calculation of James Ussher (1580–1655), archibishop of Armagh, Church of Ireland. Then he took general biology from Professor Bernal Robinson Weimer and was assigned the subject of evolution for his research paper. He concluded that Darwin had advanced "a compelling theory yet to be fully proven." A landmark of Dale's thought was changing, as it was for many others of that era. Dale said he experienced no trauma over this important new learning at Bethany.

Certain writers and intellectuals of the twenties developed some of the best literature of the century, but it was often a literature that expressed a sharp departure from traditional American values. Writers like Henry James, Ezra Pound, and T. S. Eliot lamented what they described as the "bankruptcy of civilization." Eliot's poem, *The Wasteland*, published in 1922, presented a vision of emptiness and was widely regarded as the flagship work of the age. Young Americans, wrote F. Scott Fitzgerald in *This Side of Paradise*, had "grown up to find all gods dead . . . all faith in man shaken." These writers were alienated from the new order characterized by them as hollow and bleak. Believing the humanistic spirit had been destroyed and money had become the measure of man, several, including Ernest Hemingway, simply moved out of the country to live in Paris.[28]

These writers did not represent the student view of the world at Bethany nor were they the models for Dale and his friends during those years. Dale's young intelligence was drawn not so much to the likes of Fitzgerald as to the daring of Charles Lindbergh, which lured him to Wheeling in 1927 to follow the *Lone Eagle's* progress through the public reports posted at the office of the *Wheeling News Register*. While the line of vision of many writers was trained backward longing for the old order, Dale and his Bethany friends were looking the opposite direction seeing the energy and optimism of the emerging twentieth century. They saw their world transformed by electricity, automobiles, highways, radios, motion pictures, and airplanes—and were drawn into its spirit.

When Dale returned home for Christmas in 1925, he preached his first sermon. During the second semester, he became a member of the Student Volunteer Ministerial Association and served as a student minister to the McKinleyville Mission, about three miles from Bethany. He received $5 per Sunday teaching Sunday school, preaching the sermon, and conducting the communion service. On one of those Sundays, twenty-five persons gave their confession of faith, and Dale arranged to baptize them at Bethany Memorial Church. His mother wrote to him of her great happiness for his ministry and closed her letter, "May God give you many souls for your hire," a closing she would use on every letter to him during his college years. Several decades later, Bethany Professor James Carty was lecturing at an air force base in Florida when he was approached by a man who announced he was from McKinleyville, West Virginia, and a long time ago had been baptized by "a big man reported to be a football player from Bethany." As it turned out he was one of the twenty-five baptized by Dale that Sunday during his time as the student minister.[29]

In the spring of 1926, he served a student pastorate in Allison, Pennsylvania, a congregation of about fifty members in the Coke region, which was a mission of the United Christian Missionary Society. Ministerial students were the only students at Bethany allowed to have a car, and the rules governing their use were strict. Dale borrowed $60 from his Beta fraternity brother, Forrest H. Kirkpatrick, to buy a Model-T Ford. Because of the slanted location of the gas tank, he sometimes had to back over a hill when he was low on fuel.

That summer found Dale in St. Charles, Missouri, working for his Grandfather Grubbs and uncles to earn enough money to return to

Bethany. The Grubbs family, Dale often said, nearly built old St. Charles. On weekends, he went to Sportsman's Park to see the Cardinals and Browns play baseball, watching two of his heroes, George Sissler and Rogers Hornsby. It was the year the Cardinals won the World Series.

The next two years, including summers (1927–1928), he was student minister at the Christian Church in Smithfield, Ohio, a Disciples

Dale in 1928

congregation of 119. He still drove the Model-T Ford from college to church. When he first arrived in Smithfield, the county fair was in progress. A hundred-yard dash was advertised with a huge turkey as the prize. Track season had just ended at Bethany, and Dale was in top shape so he decided to enter. A large group was competing, and just before the race began Dale had fears of finishing last and embarrassing the congregation. Dale won the race, and no one was within ten yards of him. "Parson," said the local constable, "we're going to arrest you for speeding." He rented a room in Smithfield from Mr. and Mrs. Rickey (Mother Rickey) and lived on the turkey he won for a good part of that summer.[30]

Dale's father sent him $35 per month to help with expenses. After carrying one of the checks in his pocket for some time before cashing it, Dale noticed in the Wheeling paper that the Farmer's Bank and Trust in Palm Beach had closed which meant he could not cash the check. He later learned from his father that he had indeed removed his money from the bank a few days before it closed but left $35 to cover the check. It was of course too late. In 2002, Dale still had the check, a reminder, he said, of "the fruits of procrastination."

In addition to his student pastorates, Dale found time to be an active participant in campus activities. He was president of his sophomore class, vice president and then president of the Student Volunteer Ministerial Association which had forty-eight members during his junior year. He was also captain of the football team, a member of the baseball and track teams, member of the Athletic Board of Control, member of the debate team, member of Beta Theta Pi, all while he dated his girlfriend, Ruth Ann Dye, from Hundred, West Virginia. While still a freshman, the president of the Beta fraternity, Forrest Kirkpatrick, asked Dale to supervise the house while he was away. Kirkpatrick warned in part, "Alumni who might drop in should be entertained, but you must insist on their obeying all rules of good conduct, and, above all, if you have any trouble with anyone, throw them out and think about it afterwards."[31] Another exchange of correspondence involving Forrest Kirkpatrick related to Dale's hospitalization with a mild case of typhoid fever contracted from drinking water from an old well at the fraternity house. Kirk, as the brothers knew him, wrote to Dale's parents informing them of his condition. In her eloquent style Leah responded, "Thank you for your kind letter telling us of Dale's sickness . . . It is just like Dale to tell us nothing about it until it was all over but I guess perhaps that was the best way . . . Dale seems to think Bethany is the 'stuff' and we are happy he likes it so well and has such fine friends there. Please express our sincere appreciation to all of Dale's friends who helped him pass away the unpleasant hours he spent in the hospital."[32]

Among his many Bethany friends were Dwight Stevenson, Clarence Schnars, and Bill Starn, all of whom would attend Yale Divinity School with him, Don Salmon who would become secretary of evangelism at the UCMS, Virgil Elliott who became president of Milligan College, Hollis Turley, Carl Hammil, Bob Roe, Paul Neel, and a host of others. These were strong friendships lasting a lifetime.

Dale's great passion in college was athletics. It was the golden age of sports with names like Babe Ruth, Jack Dempsey, Bobby Jones, and Red Grange capturing the sports headlines. College football was for the first time an exciting national spectator sport. Dale played baseball his freshman and senior years and ran track and played football all four years. He was the starting first baseman and right fielder on the fourteen-man varsity baseball team which compiled a seven and two record in his freshman year. The Bethany Athletic Board of Control, for budgetary reasons, dropped intercollegiate baseball and tennis during his second year.

Football then became his favorite sport in college. Furman Nuss, the Bethany football coach, usually fielded a team of thirty-five to forty-five

Dale as football
captain, 1928

DALE FIERS, Captain

players. In the fall of 1925, Dale Fiers appeared on his roster and was the
only man, according to the yearbook, "to play every minute of every
game that year." Although the team did not have a winning record, Dale's
personal performance during those years has always ranked as one of the
finest in the entire 107-year history of Bethany College football. From
1925 to 1928, Bethany played against such teams as Fordham, University
of Pittsburgh, Canisius, Westminster, Geneva, and Carnegie Tech. There
were many outstanding moments in his Bethany career such as his
eighty-yard touchdown on the opening play of the game against
Duquesne University, the sixty-yard touchdown involving Dale and Paul
"Hump" Neel in the game against West Virginia Wesleyan, and a fifty-
two-yard touchdown against Allegheny involving the same two players.
The press nicknamed him the "Plunging Parson," and the *Pittsburgh
Gazette* wrote of him, "Captain Dale Fiers, Bethany's preacher-fullback,

among other things, talks about hell on Sundays and gives opposing teams a firsthand glimpse of it the following Saturday when he bolts through the line like a baited bull."[33] Another sportswriter in Pittsburgh observed that same year: "Had Fiers been playing on the team of a large school last year, he would have been the topic for many a story as he displayed a flashy brand of ball against all opponents. Against Washington & Jefferson College, which had one of the best lines in the country, Fiers broke away time and again. Against Wittenberg College, champions of the Buckeye Athletic Conference, Fiers displayed a wonderful game, and the Wittenberg officials were at a loss to know why he received so little recognition."[34]

No doubt had Dale played football for a large school with a winning record, he would have been the subject of extensive national news coverage. But he chose instead to study for the ministry and play football at Bethany College. In his senior year, he was voted the Tri-State Conference Athlete of the Year for his performance in football, baseball, and track. He was among the first inductees into the Bethany College Athletic Hall of Fame and is still recognized as one of the all-time greatest fullbacks in the college's history, some old timers would argue in Ohio Valley sports history. As an athlete, Dale learned how much more could be achieved as a team than as an individual. He learned how to build a team, how to lead, and how to inspire. Furthermore, he learned how to coach. Historian Lester McAllister once noted that Dale, in a sense, "coached" the Disciples through their later restructure experience.[35]

June 11, 1929, arrived much too quickly. The Bethany years passed swiftly, and graduation day was suddenly at hand. On Class Day, June 10, Dale was called upon to preside at the "Planting the Evergreen" ceremony. Dwight Stevenson read the class oration, and Ruth Ann Dye read the class will. At 8:00 A.M. the next morning, Dale, having successfully completed the four-year course of study, was one of seven candidates (Edgar Bell, Dale

First pastorate, Shadyside Christian Church, men's class; Dale is second from the far right

Brock, Larue Brown, Dale Fiers, Arthur Markly, Dwight Stevenson, and Thomas Walker) ordained into the Christian ministry at the Old Bethany Meeting House. The elders on that occasion were Irvin Taylor Green, Ebenezzer Lee Perry, Henry Newton Miller, and Andrew Leitch. The presiding minister was Reverend Robert Beck who read the charge.[36]

> As you enter the service of the church, I charge that you be careful students and faithful proclaimers of the truth and grace of the Gospel of Christ . . . The ever-increasing background of our life lends reach and challenge to the work of the preachers. Live the life. Good behavior remains the great interpreter of the basic tenets of spiritual things. Prudent conduct, allows one to be known and trusted of all . . . The needs of those in stress and joy will come to you . . . Respond with helpfulness. May the spirit guide and keep you.[37]

President Cloyd Goodnight followed with the ordination prayer.

At 10:30 A.M., President Goodnight presided at the degree-awarding ceremony for the fifty-six seniors, forty-three of whom had arrived together as freshmen in 1925. The commencement address was delivered by Myers Y. Cooper, governor of Ohio and a leading Disciples layman. Reverend William H. Fields, class of '01 and pastor of First Christian Church in Wheeling, delivered the benediction. Two years later he would officiate at Dale's wedding.

Dale had accepted the call as pastor of Shadyside (Ohio) Christian Church and was to begin his ministry following graduation. George and Leah Fiers had made the long trip from Florida to attend their son's commencement. The next day they shared their good-byes, Leah and George beginning their journey home to Florida and Dale commencing his journey in ministry. When they came to the intersection of Highways 88 and 40, his parents turned left and he turned right. "It was," Dale remembered, "a long and lonely moment."[38]

The First Pastorate: Shadyside, Ohio

On April 28, John Jeffers convened an official meeting of the board of the Christian Church in Shadyside, Ohio. A proposal was presented to the board to "extend to Brother Dale Fiers a call to the pastorate of Shadyside Christian Church with a salary of $1,750 per year, not to include parsonage." The motion to approve was made by C. Wells Rodefer and passed unanimously. In true Disciples fashion, the congregation conducted its own search, screened its own candidates, and selected Dale as their minister by democratic vote. Few candidates, however, receive unanimous votes! Dale's successor at Shadyside, for example, was called with a vote of eleven supporting, two opposed, and four abstentions. Delighted with the outcome of his own call, Dale arranged to lease a room from Mr. and Mrs. Clarence R. Gillespie, who were residing in the church parsonage.[39]

The congregation had a resident membership of 198 plus twenty-five nonresidents with an average Sunday school attendance of 255 when Dale arrived in June 1929. When he left two years later, the resident membership reported to the yearbook was 340 with fifty nonresidents and an average Sunday school membership of three hundred. There were thirty-nine additions in 1930 by baptism alone, and Dale regularly taught a young men's Bible class that grew to a hundred members in less than three months.[40]

Soon after his arrival in early June, Dale organized a Vacation Bible School for the entire community. They expected and planned for seventy-five children but 350 appeared. The community graciously opened the public school to accommodate the program. "Rev-Runt" Fiers, as Elder William Lanham always called him, received high commendation for his work on this event. But his attempt later in the summer to trim the church roles to more realistically reflect the membership brought, Dale recalled, a "smoking letter that scorched me right down to the toenails."

Dale's first pastorate stands as a solid success. During his initial year, he established a monthly bulletin, redesigned Rally Day, acquired new songbooks, held two successful revivals (the first resulting in forty-one new members, twenty-seven by baptism), brought in an Anti-Saloon League speaker, launched a congregational program to financially support young persons preparing for ministry, reconfigured mission giving with four-fifths going to UCMS and one-fifth to Ohio—all in addition to the enormously successful Vacation Bible School.

He also helped the congregation extend its presence and its ministry beyond the boundaries of Shadyside. Gaines Cook, director of Christian education in Ohio, invited Dale to be director of recreation in the Summer Youth Conferences at Lakeside. It was his personal introduction to the conference movement, and the Shadyside congregation supported his efforts. The state secretary of Ohio at that time was J. J. Cahill;

Dale invited him to preach at Shadyside. In October of 1930, Dale attended the World Convention of Christian Churches in Washington, DC. The International Convention met at the same time in the same place, which provided the additional opportunity for him to attend the dedication of the newly completed National City Christian Church. The Shadyside congregation agreed to pay his expenses above the first $25. He drove to Washington with the pastor from Steubenville and stayed at the YMCA. While at Shadyside, Dale also traveled to East Liverpool, Ohio, to hear Billy Sunday, the best known evangelist of the day, Sunday preach, and, along with four friends, drove to Ohio to hear Abe Cory speak during his eight-million-dollar fund-raising campaign for the recently reorganized Pension Fund of the Christian Church. Another time, he and three colleagues rode with his good Bethany friend, Don Salmon, pastor at Bellaire. On the way, Don missed a turn and rolled his old Chevy sedan. Fortunately, it landed on its wheels, and they were able to continue the trip uninjured. As the car rolled Dale remembered wondering if his insurance premiums were current. Clearly, his view of ministry was never parochial. The context for his ministry was always the church universal, always ecumenical, always a church of multiple manifestations.[41]

Dale claimed never to have doubted ministry, but while at Shadyside he questioned if he was the right material. He remembered experiencing disturbing inner thoughts and wondered if he was qualified for the high calling. Mrs. Gillespie, Dale's landlady, remembered him being up all night praying about matters that troubled him. While experiencing this inner struggle, he heard a visiting Presbyterian minister preach on the subject. "You never know," he counseled, "what can happen when you commit your life to ministry. Leave yourself open to God's spirit!" The struggle passed. Dale said he learned three things at Shadyside: how to evangelize, how to preach, and that he needed more education.[42]

Undoubtedly, the most important event for Dale at Shadyside was meeting his future wife, Betty Chute Kunz. His old Bethany teammate, Bob Roe, who would become a Hall of Fame coach, was dating Esther Werner of Wheeling. Bob invited Dale to be the blind date for Esther's cousin, Betty, to which Dale agreed. The two couples attended a movie together at the new Capitol Theater in Wheeling. Dale learned that Betty was secretary to the principal of Wheeling High School and for the superintendent of schools. He found himself smitten by this lovely young woman with a spunky personality and beautiful singing voice. The blind date at the Capitol Theater was the beginning of a two-year courtship.

Betty's maternal grandparents, Benjamin and Elizabeth Fischer Kunz, were born in Meinisberg, Switzerland, and migrated to the United States in the 1870s. A mistake by the New York immigration authorities routed them to Wheeling by rail, along with a number of other immigrants, instead of their intended destination of Pittsburgh, Pennsylvania. They decided to stay in Wheeling, found a home on Eighteenth Street in the east part of the city, and proceeded to raise a family of eleven children whom Ben supported through his work as a carpenter.[43]

Her paternal grandparents, Daniel Chute and Elizabeth McGraw Chute, migrated to America from Ireland during the mid-1850s. They settled in Pittsburgh where they raised three children. Michael Daniel Chute, born in 1866, was their eldest child and only son. Although it is not known how they met, Michael Chute and Elizabeth Kunz, the seventh child of Ben and Elizabeth, were married and became the parents of two children, Dalton and Margaret. While the children were quite young, Elizabeth died following an operation, and Michael lived temporarily with his parents-in-law. While there, he married Rose Kunz, the fifth child of Ben and Elizabeth. The newlyweds took Margaret and Dalton and moved to Rhoney's Point near present-day Elm Grove. Here a daughter Laura was born in 1907 and a second daughter, Elizabeth or Betty as she would always be known, in 1909.[44]

Betty was only three months old when her father moved the family to Appledale, British Columbia, Canada, planning to homestead a land grant. Instead, he managed a little country store and post office. Betty was just three years old when her mother died in childbirth but the infant son, Benedict, survived. For the next four years, Michael Daniel Chute was both father and mother to the five children. "Living was hard and pleasures few," Betty recalled. Then in 1916, word came to the one-room schoolhouse where the Chute children were in class that their father was ill. Their teacher sounded the signal of emergency by ringing the school bell. The children ran home only to find their father had died of a heart attack. He had spent the days before his death chopping wood for winter fuel.[45]

At first it was thought the five Chute children, brought to Wheeling by train soon after their father's death, would be placed in an orphanage, but the Kunz family decided it would be better to divide the children among members of the family. Edward Kunz, the eldest of Ben and Elizabeth's children, was married to Louisa Barbara Kindelberger. They had lost a child at birth and were unable to have more. They took seven-year-old Betty to raise and legally adopted her as their own daughter. Betty Chute became Betty Kunz. They were excellent parents who loved Betty immensely, a love Betty returned in full measure.

Betty and Dale dated regularly throughout the remainder of 1929, all of 1930 and the early months of 1931. It cost five cents to cross the Bellaire-Wheeling toll bridge, causing Dale to surmise he had paid enough toll fees to own half-interest in the bridge. He maintained he spent all that money because of the difficult time he had convincing Betty to marry him. Dale often brought her to his Sunday evening service at Shadyside, each time asking her to sing a solo. He was so taken by her

Dale and Betty's wedding, July 14, 1931

beauty and talent that twice he forgot to take the evening offering. One of the elders reminded Dale of this oversight, "Preacher, if you ever expect to support a wife you'd better remember to take the offering."[46]

Dale informed the Shadyside Church board in April 1931 that he planned to resign effective June 1 to marry Betty Kunz and to continue his education at Yale Divinity School. A month before the wedding, Dale traveled to New Haven where he secured two part-time jobs, one preaching on weekends at Fort Trumbull Beach Community Church in Milford, Connecticut, and the other teaching a course in Old Testament and coaching at a historic boys' prep institution, Hopkins Grammar School. In addition, Yale had awarded him a three-year scholarship. The venture seemed like a great idea to the young couple, although their families, including Dale's mother, questioned the wisdom of leaving good jobs during an economic depression in order to be students at Yale.

They were married July 14, 1931, at the First Christian Church in Wheeling at 8:30 A.M. with a hundred friends and relatives present as witnesses. Bob Roe was the best man, Esther Werner, the maid of honor, and Reverend William H. Fields officiated, the same pastor who several years earlier baptized Betty. Set in place that day was a marriage bond between Dale and Betty that would fuel their lives for nearly seven decades. Immediately after the ceremony, the couple climbed into Dale's old Essex and began their sixty-seven-year journey together—first stop Yale.[47]

CHAPTER THREE

Yale to Euclid Avenue 1931–1951

Yale Divinity School

Yale Divinity School was a watershed for Dale Fiers. By his own reckoning, he arrived at Yale a classic conservative Disciple, although never a literalist or independent. He left by self-definition a "neo-orthodox Disciple." Shortly after completing his studies in New Haven, he attended an annual ministers' institute at Lakeside, Ohio. The speaker was Edwin Lewis, renowned Drew University theologian, seminary dean, and editor of *The Abington Bible Commentary*. These lectures by Lewis served to crystallize Dale's Yale leanings, advancing him toward a new theological vocabulary and a more complex faith identity.[1]

Such change did not come easily. There was a time during his years at Yale when he found himself wrestling with theological questions and with the fundamental nature of ministry. Late one winter night in New Haven after the library had closed, Dale was walking across the snow-laden quadrangle, reflecting on his inner disquiet. Almost to his car, he stopped, turned, and for a few moments stood looking at the chapel bathed in the light of the full moon suspended above it. He recalled in that instant experiencing an illumination that transcended his internal ferment. The inner discord would never return.[2]

In September of 1931 there were forty-one Disciples among the 266 students enrolled at Yale Divinity School—more than any other of the twenty-seven denominations represented in the student body that year. Disciples colleges were prominent among the 204 undergraduate feeder schools. Yale Divinity counted ten students from Bethany, six from Phillips, four from Cotner, three from TCU, three from Drake, three from Butler, two from Lynchburg, and one from Transylvania. Bethany College alone provided more students than any school in the country except Yale itself. The growing trend of Disciples attending Yale, coupled with the fact that three of Dale's close Bethany friends—William Starn, Clarence Schnars, and Dwight Stevenson—were among them, was a major influence on his decision to seek admission. Dale had initially harbored some doubt about "making it" at Yale, but Bill Starn counseled him to put those fears aside and "go on faith."[3]

Irvin T. Green of Bethany wrote enthusiastically to Dean Luther Weigle at Yale Divinity School, "I have the best Bethany news you have heard for a long time. Dale Fiers, Shadyside, Ohio, has just left my study with the request that I write you with regard to his coming to Yale next year. In my judgment, he has the best prospects of making a preacher than any Bethany man has had in ten years."[4] In February 1931, Bethany President Cloyd Goodnight wrote Weigle, concurring with Green and adding that he believed "Fiers would make a real preacher . . . he is a big, robust, fine looking chap, at ease in public address, with a good command of English."[5] Later, Dale received a letter from Dean Luther Weigle informing him the Committee on Admissions had "passed favorably on [his] application for admission."[6]

Admissions standards were undergoing a substantial change at the time of Dale's decision. One year before he enrolled, the Divinity School, for the first time in its history, implemented a selective enrollment policy requiring, among other things, that all entering students have a BA degree. It also limited the incoming class to one hundred persons. In the years that followed, it was not uncommon for one-third to one-half of those who applied to be denied admission.[7] Under these new standards, Dale's admittance was more than a routine event. Furthermore, the year of Dale's enrollment, women were admitted for the first time, and the first two to be admitted graduated in Dale's Class of 1935.[8] At the fiftieth reunion of his graduating class in 1985, Dean Leander Keck announced, by way of contrast, that fifty-one percent of the incoming class was female.

During the early 1930s, the largest percentage of Yale Divinity students were from denominational colleges west of the Ohio River. They were generally white males in their twenties, liberal arts graduates of church-related colleges who left small-town backgrounds to attend seminary in the city. Most of their fathers were farmers, ministers, tradesmen, or owners of small businesses. They were raised in the church, religiously active in college, maintained their denominational connection while in divinity school, and then returned to their denomination. This profile of the divinity school student population would prevail in theological schools until the late 1960s.[9] Dale embodied the profile in nearly every respect.

Luther Allan Weigle became dean of Yale Divinity School in 1928, a position he would hold for twenty-one years. A Lutheran, Weigle was one of the editors of the *Interpreters Bible* and the revised standard version of the Bible. He was interested in the lives of the students and a great lecturer. Dale remembered him as a "tremendous teacher." He came from a professorial background rather than the parish ministry, and he came with a vision of raising the educational standards of the divinity school to a level equal with other Yale departments. Weigle began with the infrastructure. In collaboration with James R. Angell, president of Yale, Weigle arranged for the divinity school to share in university resources and helped raise several million dollars to build a new Georgian Colonial quadrangle on Prospect Street. The plan included administrative, classroom, library, chapel, and dormitory buildings in addition to a refectory and gymnasium.[10]

He then turned his attention to the curriculum to be mastered by students. From the mid-nineteenth century, most divinity school curricula were organized around four general themes: theology, church history, the Bible, and the practice of ministry.[11] Divinity schools then fit these themes into two broad functions of ministry—practice and theory—but without structural means of integrating the two. The task of correlation was left to the students.[12]

Weigle's enthusiastic commitment to a practical or vocational orientation led him to develop a tightly systemized program. The Yale curriculum in 1931 was designed on a vocational track system offering six vocational groups with supervised fieldwork in a supportive form of ministry. Students in all six groups were required to elect courses in theological, historical, and biblical fields. Dean Weigle defended the heavy vocational orientation of the Yale program by pointing to its focus on contemporary issues facing ministers; to the opportunity it afforded to specialize in a particular type of ministry; and to the freedom it provided students to integrate the curricular offerings into a practical preparation for their own career choice in ministry.[13]

The Bulletin of Yale Divinity School, which Dale encountered in 1931 contained a listing of nine fields of study and six vocational groups from which he was obliged to choose. Dale paid the $150 tuition and resolved to study Vocational Group A, preaching ministry and pastoral service. By selecting this track, he had to demonstrate competence in the English Bible and English composition and complete eighteen courses selected from the other eight fields. Happily, Dale's selection of preaching ministry and pastoral service brought him under the distinguished tutelage of several intellectual giants in American seminary education. Included in this company were Roland Herbert Bainton in church history, Halford

Edward Luccock in homiletics, Kenneth Scott Latourette in church missions, H. Richard Niebuhr in Christian ethics, and Luther Allan Weigle in the psychology of religion.[14]

Within this eminent group of professors, Halford Luccock was the one who had the greatest influence on Dale and the one with whom Dale formed the closest bond. Luccock, a Methodist, was a jolly person with a good sense of humor. He was of medium height and build, friendly, interested in his students, and a prolific reader. Dale recalled visiting the private study in the Luccock home and viewing his card file containing twenty-two thousand sermon illustrations gleaned from his extensive reading, a habit he repeatedly urged upon all of his students. Dale also remembered with appreciation the class sessions designed for analyzing and criticizing student sermons. Luccock always found something positive in every sermon and would not leave a student feeling devastated. Dale was so impressed with Dr. Luccock that he decided if he ever had a son he would consider naming him "Halford." When mother Leah heard this news she advised Dale not to do it because, in her opinion, the name would inevitably be shortened to Hal Fiers and would be deliberately abridged or heard incorrectly as "Hell Fires."[15]

Roland Bainton, a Congregationalist, open and warm in personality, was the most popular member of the Yale Divinity School faculty. Dale, well immersed in church history from his Bethany years, chose the common practice of frequently attending Bainton's more renowned lectures instead of taking the classes, thereby allowing more time for other coursework. Bainton's special lectures, such as "Abelard and Eloise," were publicized in advance and students and guests alike filled the lecture hall.

During his 1933 middler year, Dale enrolled in systematic theology taught by Dr. Douglas Clyde Macintosh, who was then Dwight Professor of Theology. This was an important course in Dale's faith journey, a journey that never reaches full resolution for those who take faith seriously.

Here Dale was exposed to the scholarly study of theology and to critical thinking of the first order, although there were moments of lesser order. He remembered, for example, Macintosh teaching that, "With the Christ of faith idea you have the essence of Christianity even without the historical Jesus." It was, Macintosh declared, "the irreducible minimum." But in another class, Dale mirthfully recalled, the professor referred to the same idea as "the expandable maximum."[16]

Macintosh, a ruddy Scots-Canadian, required his students to set forth a systematic statement of their understanding of the fundamental aspects of the Christian religion. In response to Macintosh, as a means of expressing his personal credo, Dale employed a dialogue format within a fictitious setting of a board of examination for ordination asking all the big questions about God, evil, Christ, baptism, the Bible, and faith. In a twenty-seven-page narrative, he outlined a clear and informed statement of his theological beliefs as a twenty-five-year-old seminarian attempting to integrate new learning into an ever-evolving personal theological frame.

Referring to himself as "George Allen" in the paper, Dale began with a brief synopsis of his faith and belief offered to the examining board:

"I believe in God as a personal being, who is the creator and sustainer of the universe; a God great enough and good enough to meet the needs of man.

"I believe that Jesus is the Son of God and the Saviour of the world; that in Him we find the true moral, social, and religious ideal; that he is the revelation of what God is.

"I believe in the Holy Spirit as the power and influence of God's revelation working in the life of the world, bringing it to a conviction of sin and leading it into ever expanding avenues of new truth.

"I believe that man is created in the image of God in the sense that he is an essentially free moral agent who can feel, will, and act; that he is responsible for his life and conduct.

"I believe in the immortality of the human soul; that there is a conscious existence of the individual after bodily death.

"I believe that the church is the body of Christ; the church is the agency through which Christian religion is perpetuated in the world; that its main purpose is the accomplishment of the mission of Jesus, namely to bring about the establishment of the Kingdom of God.

"I believe in the historic sacraments of the church, baptism and the Lord's Supper; that baptism is a highly spiritual and symbolic act depicting the death and burial of the individual to the old life out of Christ and the resurrection to walk in the newness of life in Christ; moreover, that it is an expression of inner commitment to the faith and life of Jesus; that the Lord's Supper is a memorial to the ministry of Jesus and the hope that we have in Him.

"I believe that the Bible is a record of the revelation of God in life and action; that it is a rich source of spiritual guidance and worthy of the deepest devotion, study, and profound loyalty."[17]

The story continues in narrative form with several members of the examining board raising questions with the candidate. A brief sampling of selected questions accompanied by Dale's response through "George Allen" allows us to peer more deeply into the fundamental beliefs of a young man at the seminary stage of his theological development.

EXISTENCE OF GOD

Question: "What reasons do you find for believing in the existence of God?"

Answer: "I do not feel that the existence of God can be absolutely demonstrated, neither can it be disproved. That God exists is the necessary presupposition of theology . . . I have been impressed with the cosmological argument . . . positing an adequate first cause. Since this universe has produced human personality, there must be a cause that is as great as the human mind and personality and presumably greater. That first cause is God. I believe God *is* because God is the only reasonable explanation for the universe and the meaning of life."[18]

EVIL

Question: "Do you believe in a personal devil?"

Answer: "No."

Question: "How do you account for the evil in the world?"

Answer: "I must admit there is much about evil that puzzles me. I accept the reality of evil in all of its [manifestations], moral, mental, and physical, not as the work of some perverted cosmic being but as incidental to the kind of world we live in. If [human beings] have freedom of choice, there must of necessity be the possibility of choosing the wrong thing. The same fire that keeps us warm in winter may burn us to death if it is not used properly. Man can do much to eliminate evil; it is certainly not God's will that evil should flourish. Despite all [human] effort there is much pain, suffering, sickness, and death. How shall we face it? Without religious faith, it seems to me that the problem of evil remains insoluble. While much of evil is regrettable and seemingly unuseful, faith in God enables us to overcome evil."[19]

VIRGIN BIRTH

Question: "Do you believe in the Virgin Birth of Christ?"

Answer: "I do not consider it of vital importance to believe in Jesus as the Christ, and moreover, I feel it must not be made an issue but left entirely to one's opinion and judgment. I believe the story of the Virgin Birth is an attempt to explain the uniqueness of Jesus. It is not authentic as history but is valid as an appreciation."[20]

RESURRECTION OF JESUS

Question: "Do you believe in the resurrection of Jesus as a suspension of natural law?"

Answer: "I think that dogmatism at this point is exceedingly unfortunate. I do not accept the commonly held view of the physical resurrection of Jesus, but I cannot escape the conviction that there was objective validity in the resurrection of Jesus and in the experiences of his Disciples who were reported to have seen Him after His death. I do not think it necessary to regard this as wholly [outside] the realm of natural process even while granting its uniqueness. I can go no further than to say, 'I believe, help thou mine unbelief.'"[21]

JESUS, THE SON OF GOD

Question: "In what sense do you think Jesus to be the Son of God?"

Answer: "I believe that Jesus was *the* Son of God, in the sense that the divine quality and value of His life was His distinguishing characteristic. His real sonship is evident not from any physical characteristics but in the filial character of His spiritual relationship with God."[22]

BAPTISM

Question: "Do you think baptism is necessary to the salvation of the individual?"

Answer: "No. I think that view of baptism would involve something of a magical efficacy in the external rite, which is not true to the mind of Christ or compatible with truth. I prefer to think of baptism as a symbol of personal commitment to Christ. It becomes a thing of great significance and value, not in itself, but as the outward expression of an inward experience."[23]

SOCIAL GOSPEL

Question: "Are you an advocate of the social gospel?"

Answer: "I do not believe the social gospel is separate or distinct from the gospel but an integral part of it. I certainly believe in the social emphasis of the gospel message as a means of bringing about the Kingdom of God on earth and that it calls not only for talk but concrete expression."[24]

Strong pastors have the ability to articulate their faith. It was one of Dale's many gifts to be able to express something so personal in a forthright, honest, and succinct fashion. No double meanings, no hidden meanings, no euphemisms, and no ambiguities—just a simple, straightforward statement of faith. Dale's discourse actually contained questions on eighteen different theological subjects, with considerable interplay between the questioners and the candidate. The short list of seven included here, even with responses abbreviated, illustrates his command of theology, his command of self-expression, and a natural struggle to overcome doubt, along with some of the pain Dale felt standing in the quadrangle snow late at night looking at the chapel bathed in moonlight, wondering about the essence of ministry. In a telling comment included in the preface to his paper we learn that Dale's faith was being "reconstructed": "I must add a word of appreciation for the inspiring influence of Douglas Clyde Macintosh under whose guidance and instruction I have been able to re-evaluate and reconstruct my Christian faith with a deepening sense of its eternal worth."[25]

Dale studied social ethics under Jerome Davis, a child of missionary parents in Japan, an ordained man of faith, unorthodox in his ideas and in his teaching. He was an idealist who expressed the depression-generated thought that people could find some better way of living together than dog-eat-dog capitalism. A new cooperative social structure, in his view, was not an impossible dream. He was labeled a socialist by some, a communist by others, and was soon dismissed from the faculty.

Davis used the pedagogical technique of placing a copy of *The New York Times* on each student's desk, then asking them to read it and respond to the question, "To what kind of world are you preparing yourselves to minister?" He once took Dale's entire class on a field trip to New York City where they slept three nights in a flophouse with twelve hundred homeless persons. They ate in the soup kitchens, visited people (three of whom thought they were Jesus) in psychiatric hospitals, interacted with institutionalized individuals on Roosevelt Island, visited the morgue where they saw the bodies of babies that had been fished out of the East River, and talked with residents in the box houses of the Battery Mission. Dale affirmed this course made him conscious of social issues at a depth he had never before conceived.[26]

He studied the New Testament with the Scots-Presbyterian professor, John Young Campbell; Old Testament under the tall, lanky George Dahl with whom Dale claimed to have done his worst work in seminary; and worship with Henry Hallam Tweedy, a fastidious and classic New England professor with a Van Dyke beard. A former missionary to India and the only Disciple on the faculty, Dr. John Clark Archer, taught the course on comparative religions. Dale found him difficult to know, not necessarily unapproachable but a bit aloof.

Paul Herman Vieth, a Congregationalist, was professor of religious education and another key influence on Dale. A stocky man with a brush haircut, lively personality, and warm demeanor, he tried often and unsuccessfully to convince Dale to shift his major to Christian education. Dale prepared a thirty-five-page research paper for Dr. Vieth during the spring of 1934. It was entitled, "The Unified Program and the Local Church," and became an important reference point for Dale in his subsequent pastorates. Dr. Vieth was highly complimentary of the effort, noting, "This is a *superior* paper—the kind one does not often get as part of the requirements in a single course—I like especially your historical approach."[27]

The professor of public speaking was Hubert Greaves, a heavyset man with a powerful voice, who taught Dale to "speak from the abdomen." Dale took this course as a middler in 1933 and won both the

Downes prize—$30 (the student who attains the highest proficiency in the public reading of the Scriptures) and the Mersick prize—$75 (to the member of the class in Homiletics and Public Speaking adjudged by the professors to have shown the most marked improvement). The shy student on the back row in a Kankakee classroom faded into history. And how pleased his high school teacher, Emily Keyes, would be to learn the result of her caring nurture.[28]

During the middler year, Dale and Betty lived at 699 Forest Road but resided the next two years at 301 Orchard where Bill Starn had lived prior to graduation. Betty studied music with the wife of the dean of the School of Music, sang with the New Haven light opera, and audited courses at Yale University. In addition to the heavy load of coursework, Dale performed his ministry as a student pastor at Fort Trumbull Beach Union Chapel and as a part-time faculty member and coach at Hopkins Grammar School. He also found time, probably at the urging of Luccock, to read some of the novels of Hemingway, Faulkner, Steinbeck, and Fitzgerald. For Betty and Dale, it was a period of both significant challenge and significant growth.

One substantial challenge during his seminary years was the fall semester of 1934. That September he enrolled in Christian ethics with H. Richard Neibuhr, the expansion of Christianity with Kenneth Scott Latourette, and the psychology of religion with Luther Allan Weigle. It was his final push to complete the requirements for graduation. Each of the three professors assigned major research projects and all three were due by mid-December. Latourette, an American Baptist, was a large man, accessible and an excellent lecturer, who was busy writing a history of Christian missions. Niebuhr, a member of the Reformed Church, was a forceful and popular lecturer with unusual gesticulations. He was hard at work on his book, *The Social Sources of Denominationalism*. An autographed copy is still on the shelf of Dale's library.

Fort Trumbull Beach Chapel, near Yale

For Latourette's class, Dale prepared a thirty-five-page research paper, "The Conflict between Christianity and Gnosticism," in which he observed, "Gnosticism as a self-consistent development from a definite beginning is not to be found. It is rather a tendency which began in certain ideas or notions and which was shaped by the religious and philosophical conditions that surrounded it." In Weigle's course, Dale penned a thirty-three-page research paper on "The Place of Pastoral Psychology in the Work of the Ministry." The research led Dale to the conclusion that the "personal approach to the problem of human adjustment in the work of the minister has strong appeal . . . especially in the light of all the intriguing discoveries and theories of the leaders in psychiatry, psychoanalysis and kindred movements." It was his further judgment that religion was "given a new significance as an integrative force in the development of personality," but he was quick to caution that a minister should not "become so engrossed in the problems of individuals that he may forget the importance of the prophetic office and the moral demand for the changing of social conditions. . . . If ministry is to reach its full development," he asserted, "it must combine both the personal and the social."[29]

Drawing on the writings of Westermark, Sorley, Rogers, and Hume, Dale wrote a twenty-two-page treatise on "Westermark's Theory of Ethical Relativity" for H. Richard Neibuhr's course on Christian ethics. All three papers were delivered on time, December 11, 12, and 17, essentially completing Dale's seminary requirements. Latourette scrawled the word "Excellent" across the front of the paper on Gnosticism. Weigle awarded Dale an A in his course on the psychology of religion, and H. Richard Neibuhr attached the following note to Dale's research paper on Westermark: "I am very much pleased with this paper and have no hesitancy in rating it an A job. I have neither criticisms nor suggestions for improvement to offer. I hope you will greatly enjoy your work at

Hamilton. Farewell!" It must have been a joyous Christmas in the Fiers' household that year. He had completed the work on schedule, received solid marks, had a pastorate awaiting him in Ohio, and only needed to tie up a few details to graduate in June of 1935.[30]

High Street Church of Christ: Hamilton, Ohio

Gaines Cook was a regular visitor to the Disciples Divinity House at Yale. He provided denominational connection and nurture for the growing number of Disciples students attending the seminary. Through him, Dale learned the Reverend G. Webster Moore had announced during the summer of 1934 that he was planning to retire as pastor of High Street Church of Christ in Hamilton, Ohio. Dale was invited to interview for the position by Harry Helwig, chair of the Pulpit Committee and destined to be a future colleague with Dale at United Christian Missionary Society. The congregational interview and visit proved successful, and Dale was offered a salary of $1,300 per year plus parsonage to become the pastor. He accepted and agreed to begin the ministry in September 1935.[31]

The Great Depression was at its zenith. Economic life had broken down and had created, in the words of T. H. Watkins, "a social horror . . . which often ripped middle class families to shreds."[32] The suffering, dislocation, and hurt inflicted upon untold millions is difficult to grasp. Arthur M. Schlesinger Jr. caught some of the pathos in his writing, *The Crises of the Old Order:* "March 3, 1933. Across the country, the banks of the nation had gradually shuttered their windows and locked their doors," he wrote. He proceeded to describe the American economy as seemingly coming to a stop. "The fog of despair," he said, "hung over the land." One out of every four American workers was unemployed. Factories stood silent. He described families who "slept in tarpaper shacks and tin-lined caves and scavenged like dogs for food in the city dump." There were marchers in the streets and violence in the countryside.[33]

Economic slumps had occurred before, but there was nothing in the American experience to match the punishing effects of the Great Depression. The people who endured the long ordeal would carry the scars all their lives. It was clearly a time in need of the healing ministry of

High Street Church of Christ, Hamilton, Ohio—Dale's first pastorate following Yale, 1935–1939

the church, but the church was also stricken by the Great Depression, presenting a challenging moment to enter ministry.

By 1932, the year of Franklin Delano Roosevelt's election, the depression was having a serious impact on Disciples congregations. Attendance was declining, offerings were down, staff was reduced, mortgages were delinquent, and salaries were lagging or not being paid at all. Due to their inability to support a full program of ministry, some congregations opted for weekend services only. Likewise, the national agencies of the church were incurring severe damage to their institutional life. By December 1932, a deficit of $1,126,952 had been accumulated at the UCMS. Income had dropped from nearly $3,000,000 in 1929 to roughly $1,400,000 in 1935, prompting then-president Stephen J. Corey to call home several missionaries from overseas. Selected agencies—the National Benevolent Association in 1933, the Board of Church Extension in 1934, and the Board of Higher Education in 1938—separated from the UCMS for reasons part financial and part polity.[34]

Positive advances were also evident among Disciples during those years. On July 1, 1935, a program of cooperation in budget making and joint promotion of causes was established and given the name "Unified Promotion." Clarence O. Hawley was appointed director of the program, and it proved to be one of the most effective creations in Disciples' institutional history. Also in 1935, the International Convention meeting in San Antonio founded the Disciples Peace Fellowship, destined to become the conscience for Disciples on world peace. And the depression sparked among Disciples congregations in general an increased sensitivity to social justice. The International Conventions of 1933 and 1934 approved messages on social justice and economic justice, asking for guarantees against unemployment and advocating old-age security.[35]

The High Street pastorate was an important four-year experience for Dale. At this Ohio congregation, he would begin to implement his newly developed understanding of the essence of ministry in the midst of conditions spawned by the Great Depression. Here he would first employ Veith's Christian education material. And it was here that he first began to wear striped trousers and a charcoal jacket as his preaching attire. Hamilton was the initial testing ground for all he had learned and for all he wanted to become. The four years at High Street shaped the grain and texture of his pastoral ministry for the next fifteen years.

Dale had accurately sized up the Hamilton situation during his interview and visit. The church building was in dire need of repair and renovation, but financial resources were in short supply. The Christian Education Program was sagging with a decline in Sunday school and Vacation Bible School attendance. Membership growth had stalled, and participation in the wider church and world mission was minimal. Beyond the effects of the Great Depression, there was an apparent lack of self-confidence, a weakening of the spirit that was eroding the ministry of the congregation. In light of these conditions, Dale decided upon seven areas of concentration for his High Street ministry: religious education, stewardship, world mission, wider church participation, development of a youth program, spiritual strengthening of the congregation, and remodeling the church building.[36]

High Street was quick to size up Dale as well. The annual report of the congregation for 1935 noted: "Mr. Fiers came from recent study at Divinity School. With his good looks, youthful vigor, and enthusiasm it was soon recognized that he was quite capable of taking over the pastoral work." The Fiers' pastorate was launched September 9, 1935.[37]

He began his ministry that September with a religious education week, an event that would continue annually. He organized banquets to honor teachers and leaders of the church school and provide training sessions to assist them with their teaching. He worked especially hard to strengthen the Vacation Bible School, which grew in his first summer to sixty-one participants.

To renew a sense of world mission, Dale established a six-week school of worldwide Christianity. The school was reinforced by a steady stream of visiting speakers, averaging one per month, and including such respected individuals as Oswald Goulter, missionary to China.

Dale believed regular exposure to the wider church was imperative to the good health of a local congregation. He helped set in place arrangements for High Street to host a district convention during his first year, and by his second year the Hamilton congregation had the largest delegation (twenty-eight) attending the district assembly, held in Harrison. Dale and several members represented the congregation at the Ohio State Assembly. When Gaines Cook and Clarence Hawley visited Hamilton to present the new program called "Unified Promotion," High Street became one of the early congregations to accept their goal and to be in full cooperation. Dale also represented the congregation at the International Convention where he served on the recommendations committee.[38]

Perhaps the biggest challenge during those depression years was to generate sufficient resources to support the ministry of the congregation. Dale organized an every-member canvas just three months after his arrival. When this did not raise enough to underwrite the budget, the church sold bonds to individual members. Other fund-raising events included ice cream festivals, rummage sales, fish fries, and quilt sales. Dale also organized a three-month stewardship campaign with one month designated for all-church tithing. The tithing experience taught him a stewardship lesson when he discovered that fifteen persons gave more than the rest of the congregation. The combined efforts bore a good result. The building debt was paid down and the building itself was renovated during his second year. When he came to High Street in 1935, the budget was $4,496 but by 1937 it had risen to $5,600—in spite of the depression.[39]

To strengthen the spiritual life of the church, Dale began, in his second month, to hold Sunday evening services and weekly prayer meetings. Added to this were Christmas Eve services, Holy Week candlelight communion services, Easter evangelistic services, and a series of eight-day preaching missions.

In 1936, Dale led in planning the eightieth anniversary celebration of the congregation's founding. In this event, he saw a grand opportunity to help the congregation regain a sense of self through its history and to restore confidence in its ministry. He organized a weeklong celebration around the theme of "The Preaching Mission of the Church." The plans included a banquet emphasizing Christian education, a banquet for all members eighty years and older, and a Homecoming Sunday to be highlighted with a historical pageant. All of these efforts had a positive effect. Membership stood at 450 when Dale arrived at High Street; by 1938 it had grown to 515. The December 1936 annual congregational report included the statement, "It is interesting to note the number of pledges in 1932 was more than doubled in 1936 and whereas only 34% were fully paid at the end of 1932, 51% were paid at the end of 1936."[40]

During his Hamilton years Dale was very active with the Youth Conference movement, teaching in many parts of the region. He was heavily involved with the local YMCA and Ministerial Association and also led in organizing a "twenty-plus" club composed of many unemployed young men who joined to help each other find jobs. But without question, the most memorable event of the Hamilton years was the birth to Betty and Dale of a daughter, Barbara Louise, born February 23, 1936.

At the November 1938 board meeting, Dale presented a letter of resignation in order to accept the pastorate of Central Church of Christ in Newark, Ohio. His resignation was received with "great regret." These had been good years, and in his letter Dale expressed confidence in the future of the church and said that he would always cherish memories of the friendliness and thoughtfulness that made their Hamilton ministry such a happy one. He preached his final sermon at High Street on Sunday, December 20, 1938.[41]

Central Church of Christ: Newark, Ohio

Reflecting on his ministry, Dale commented nostalgically about his time at Newark's Central Church of Christ. "Newark," he said, "is in my heart. It was the most satisfying moment of my ministry."[42]

Gaines Cook, once again, was the person who alerted Dale to the opportunity and urged him to go. Reverend Louis Mink had resigned in 1938 after eleven years of service to the congregation. Dale and Betty arrived January 1, 1939, to begin the labor of love they would both so

Central Church of Christ, Newark, Ohio, 1939–1945

The Fiers family, 1942

fondly remember. The young couple settled in at 133 Mount Vernon Road. Within a short time three hundred church members greeted them at a huge welcoming reception.[43] It was clearly a good match.

When the Fiers arrived in 1939, the congregation had a membership of 822, and when they left in 1945 it had grown to 1,061. The budget increased more than five-fold from $6,331 annually to $33,086 during his nearly seven years of ministry. The success was remarkable and grew essentially out of the seven-point plan for ministry Dale had employed at Hamilton. A few years later in a conversation with his predecessor, Louis Mink, Dale sought advice about the necessity of maintaining a certain Sunday school class. Reverend Mink responded with words that Dale would never forget: "Every well ordered kitchen needs a garbage can."[44]

He accelerated the youth program by organizing a CYF and a Chi Rho group of forty members. He also created a sports program for them and instituted a noonday luncheon series for young people; he also had a recreation lodge built nearby for them. During Dale's Newark years, congregational giving for outreach grew from $2,000 to $5,285 per year.[45] He placed heavy emphasis on world missions with a steady appearance of visitors from around the world and across the nation, including a living link missionary, Dr. Brady, who was serving in China. On Sunday, December 7, 1941, Dr. Brady was visiting the High Street congregation and lunched with Dale and Betty at the parsonage. Shortly after lunch, they learned of the Japanese bombing of Pearl Harbor.

Dale's keen interest in keeping the congregation informed about the wider church always caused him to urge the Newark congregation to participate in the district and state assemblies. In fact, it was during the state convention being hosted at Newark that Betty and Dale had their second child, a son, Alan Dale, born April 15, 1939. Dale recalled the great joy of announcing Alan's birth to that assembly.[46] True to his mother's wishes, he did not name his son Halford.

He served as president of the Ohio Commission on Christian Education and as president of the Licking County Ministerial Association where he helped develop a union plan of worship for the county and city. Dale invested himself enthusiastically in the development of an ecumenical approach to evangelism. There was, however, an unsuccessful attempt at a district meeting to convince a rock-ribbed Disciple of the virtues of ecumenism. "If the nearest Disciples congregation was eighteen miles away, where would you attend?" asked Dale. And the man replied, "I would go eighteen miles!"

In 1944, Dale gave leadership to the planning of a sixtieth anniversary celebration for the church, just as he had at Hamilton. It was reported to have been a grand success. Because of the crowded conditions in the church due to growth, he led an effort that year to construct a new building. A building committee was appointed, a lot acquired, and a goal of

$18,000 established for the project. The fund-raising effort actually netted $23,000 and plans for the new church were begun.

The Newark years were shadowed by World War II. On September 1, 1939, nine months to the day after the Fiers' arrival in Newark, Hitler invaded Poland and the world would never again be the same. Across Discipledom opinion was divided between neutrality and early intervention. It was soon learned that sixteen Disciples missionaries were in prisons in various parts of the world, and 460 Disciples chaplains were serving in the military. Throughout the war years, Dale, although involved in community civil defense, found that caring for the families and their sons overseas became a daily part of his ministry. Forty young men from the Central Church of Christ congregation were fighting on the battlefields of Europe and Asia. Every issue of the *Newark Christian* carried a constant reminder of the world at war. Its listing of those missing in action, wounded, home on leave or furlough brought the war right to the heart of the congregation. It was Dale's nature to reach out to these young men and to their families at home. He wrote regularly to the "Fellows" overseas letting them know the church was remembering them. In his letter dated June 8, 1942, he wrote,

> Dear Fellows,
>
> I am writing this letter to each of you to tell you about the very fine service we had last Sunday evening which was devoted to all our boys away from home.
>
> We have quite a number, about forty altogether. We were happy to have so many friends and relatives present to take part Sunday evening when we read your names and remembered you in our prayers.[47]

Dale proceeded to add two long paragraphs about happenings in the congregation and invited any suggestions the fellows might have for the improvement of their home church. Another of his letters to the fellows dated August 16, 1945, announced the end of the war.

> Dear Fellows,
>
> The war is over! While you have long since heard this, we all want you to know that we were rejoicing with you and thanking God for the victory that brings us again an opportunity to build a lasting peace.
>
> We had a great service at church last night. Over three hundred people attended to join in praise and thanksgiving. One could sense the deep mood of joy and gratitude of the congregation. As I looked over the audience, I could see many of your folks—wives, sweethearts, parents, and friends.
>
> One finds it hard to comprehend but that thing we have all been been talking about—"the post-war-world" is now upon us. We wish eagerly for the day of your permanent return home and the return of conditions which will make possible the continuation of your normal life and work.[48]

The service of Thanksgiving for the end of the war to which Dale referred was held on a Wednesday evening. It opened with the singing of the "Star Spangled Banner," a reading of an epistle to the Americans written by Dale and several colleagues, and the singing of "America, the Beautiful." Individual members offered prayers of thanksgiving, followed by Dale's own eloquent prayer.

> Accept, O God, our humble thanks for this final victory that has come to us. May we face the blessing and the problems of peace with understanding and courage. We beseech thee to comfort those who have lost loved ones in this conflict; grant the

healing presence of thy Holy Spirit to all those who have been hurt and wounded by the awful violence of war. Guide and direct us and our leaders into the paths that will make for permanent peace and abundant life for all mankind.

In the name of Jesus. Amen.[49]

Dale was granted an educational leave in the summer of 1945 to study Old Testament at Union Theological Seminary in New York. At Union he met Paul Tillich and Harry Emerson Fosdick. While at these seminars he received an invitation to become senior pastor of the famed Euclid Avenue Christian Church in Cleveland, Ohio. He and Betty decided to accept the challenge of a new ministry and made preparation to begin on October 15, 1945. They would leave Newark before several of the young men were released to come home. A large farewell gathering of five hundred persons assembled at Central Church to tell the Fiers good-bye. Dale and Betty were beloved by the congregation, and there was a deep sense of loss in their departure. Their many achievements—spiritual, community, congregational—were recited over and over again that evening. One speaker offered a reason for the deep affection they felt for Dale, "He has a genuineness about him that makes him not look like a minister!" Dale responded in his gracious and succinct way: "Whatever good has happened during our pastorate was due to the cooperation of the people, the preceding ministers, and most of all to the providence of God."[50]

Euclid Avenue Christian Church: Cleveland

The newspaper headlines offered stark contrast but all were born of love for a pastor. The *Newark Advocate and American Tribune*, the *Newark Christian* and the *News of the Brotherhood* all lauded Dale's selection and displayed pride in his appointment to one of the most prestigious of

Euclid Avenue Church of Christ, 1945–1951

Disciples congregations. Their headlines proclaimed, "A. Dale Fiers called to Cleveland," "500 Honor Rev. Fiers and Family," and "Dale Fiers Leaves October 1."[51]

The *Cleveland Plain Dealer* and Euclid Avenue Christian Church publications carried the love of a different pastor in their headlines announcing, "Newark Minister in Goldner Pulpit," "Dr. Goldner's Successor Given Hand of Fellowship," and "Fiers Named Successor to Goldner." Contained in those headlines was a challenge Dale would face throughout his Euclid Avenue ministry.[52]

Rev. Jacob H. Goldner had been minister at Euclid Avenue for forty-five years. He had come to the congregation January 1, 1900, while pursuing a seminary degree at the University of Chicago. His wife was killed in 1925 during a street celebration after the Cleveland Indians won the pennant. The church, thereafter, was his bride. The Euclid Avenue Church experienced extraordinary growth under his remarkably devout leadership, making Goldner a beloved legend to both the congregation and the city. When Dale was called to succeed him, there was understandably more sadness in the congregation over Goldner's retirement than happiness over the appointment of a successor no matter who it might have been.

The Goldners, father and son, were among the many who wrote to Dale extending a personal welcome. "Please be assured," offered Reverend Goldner, "that I am greatly pleased by our pulpit committee's decision to recommend you to our official board and congregation as my successor." Then he added, "I am glad that you plan to be in Cleveland Thursday afternoon and evening so that you may informally meet our board members. Will you kindly come to the church upon your arrival in Cleveland; and may I have the pleasure of entertaining you at dinner? This will give us ample time for questions and answers."[53] Goldner's son, Gerould, also sent a letter to Dale. "So often in times past when folks would ask me who would be my dad's successor at Cleveland Euclid Avenue Christian Church, I would in the privacy of my own thoughts hope that it might be you. You can imagine my delight when I heard you were definitely to be called."[54]

Throughout 1946, Goldner's name was carried on the front of the Sunday morning worship bulletin as minister emeritus. By 1947, Dale's second year, the word emeritus was dropped from the banner of the church paper, and Goldner was listed as one of three ministers of the congregation—A. Dale Fiers, Jacob H. Goldner, and Howard Spangler. Complexity was added to the situation by the fact that when Dale arrived in 1945 Howard Spangler was in his thirty-third year as associate minister and Martha Roudebush was in her twenty-fifth year as church secretary. Reverend Goldner was so well known and universally loved that Dale found discussing some aspect of his life and work in almost every pastoral call inescapable. Looking back on the experience, Dale reflected, "Following his ministry was a challenge. Still in my thirties, I found it a high mountain to climb."[55]

Dale loved to tell the story of Newark friends coming to visit Euclid during his early weeks as pastor. Not knowing who they were or that they were admirers of Dale, the Euclid lady seated in front of them turned to extend a warm greeting and then explained, "We have a new minister. He's not as good as our old one, but we think he is going to be all right." As late as 1968, when the congregation celebrated its 125th anniversary, the historical booklet published for the occasion labeled Dale's six-year ministry at Euclid as "Transition Years."[56]

But for Dale, it was one of the most important periods of his life, and he has always considered Euclid Avenue Christian Church the most influential congregation of his career. Thinking back on his later call to the presidency of the UCMS, Dale believed, "It never would have been extended without the opportunities and exposure my relationship to Euclid Avenue Christian Church afforded me."[57]

In the fall of 1945, Dale, Betty, Barbara, and Alan moved into their new Cleveland residence at 3331 Bradford Road. A canine pet joined the family circle in this new home and was promptly named the "Duke of Bradford." Fitting into the new congregation was at first a bit tentative for Betty because the church had been without a senior pastor's wife for twenty years. It was also a bit awkward for the church, but the women of the congregation soon embraced Betty with opportunities to participate and grow. Both Barbara and Alan were baptized at Euclid Avenue, events that gave the Euclid church a special place in the family heritage.

Dale, on the other hand, was a little intimidated at being in his first metropolitan congregation and struggled during his early months. He vividly remembered an elder, Tom Hann, taking him aside one day and saying, "Dale, you are in the big leagues now, and you are wondering if you will fail. We will not let you fail!"[58] No one, Dale admitted, could ever begin to imagine what those words meant to him. Euclid Avenue caused him to modify his concept of ministry. The congregation was filled with capable leadership, more chiefs than warriors, enough leadership, he said, "to guide a dozen churches." Many members, he discovered, could perform aspects of ministry better than he. Dale learned how to use active laypersons and has often repeated the insightful lesson taught him by the Euclid experience, "You do well to surround yourself with people smarter than you."

Some things that worked well in county seat town congregations did not work at all in large urban churches. Weekend preaching missions, for example, so successful in Hamilton and Newark were failures in Cleveland. It made no difference if the preacher was Dale or a guest, the weekends simply did not generate enough attendance to continue the practice.

One of the most controversial issues in Discipledom during the 1930s and 1940s was "open membership," a more inclusive understanding of baptism than the rigid requirement of baptism by immersion. It was a difficult choice for Disciples. If they refused open membership, they were in effect participating in the division of the Body of Christ. If they accepted open membership, they thought of themselves as approving forms of baptism not found in the New Testament. The leading journals were at opposite ends of the spectrum: *The Christian Century* strongly favored the practice of open membership and *The Christian Standard* was adamantly opposed. The *Christian Evangelist* disapproved of open membership but advocated cordial relations with congregations that adopted the practice. In 1948, the UCMS sent a questionnaire to all congregations asking their stance on the issue. Of approximately five thousand congregations, 117 of them openly declared the practice while about one thousand congregations indicated they practiced it "quietly." In an effort to modify the Euclid congregational stance on closed membership, Dale privately developed an "ecumenical membership" proposal and tested it with a local clergy club. "They peeled the bark off me," he reported. Although he did not achieve open membership at Euclid Avenue, he planted the seed that flowered under his successor, Walter McGowan, when Euclid Avenue became an open membership congregation. He did succeed in performing a membership audit that reduced the reported number of 1,815 at the time of his arrival to a yearbook total of 1,400 when he left.

One idea that proved successful and was readily received at Euclid was a handsome new church newsletter. Volume One, Number One appeared November 16, 1945, one month after his arrival.[59] It announced his first new initiative for 1946, an expansion of the Sunday morning religious education program of worship and study with the introduction of the most modern visual aids into the teaching program of the church. Dale believed the cornerstone of an informed and vital congregation was Christian education, and it was the first program he chose to rekindle in each of his three Ohio pastorates. At Euclid, he was assisted in this effort by a laywoman, Mildred Jarvis, who subsequently moved onto a professional career in religious education with UCMS.

One of the most poignant moments of his Euclid ministry was the commemoration of the fiftieth anniversary of Jacob Goldner's ministry. The celebration was scheduled for January 8, 1950. But on December 30, Reverend Goldner suffered a massive heart attack. Dale went immediately to see him, "I've finished my sermon," Goldner reported. "It would have been a great day—will you preach it for me?" Later that day Goldner died, and the following week, Dale, true to his word, preached Goldner's sermon.[60] The sermon ended with the words, "the epitaph on the tombstone of an Alpine climber reads, 'He died climbing.' Let mine be, 'He died preaching.'"

Dale's many achievements at Euclid Avenue included the establishment of the nation's first Christian Women's Fellowship. Assisting him was the exceptionally talented Freda Putnam who was president of the group and later named president of the International Christian Women's

The Fiers family, 1948

Fellowship. The creation of the congregation's first board of deaconesses was another accomplishment of his ministry at Euclid.

From 1947 to 1950, Dale led Euclid Avenue in its congregational role as part of the three-year denominational program, "Crusade for a Christian World." At that time, it was the largest program ever attempted by Disciples. Seeking to catch the spirit of the postwar era, it was designed to seize upon the revival of interest in religion. The program called for the establishment of two hundred new congregations, recruitment of persons for ministry, growth in church membership, and $14,000,000 to be raised for support of these goals. Euclid Avenue's share of this goal was $40,000, and Dale successfully raised that amount. The whole experience deepened the congregation's appreciation for the wider church.

Commenting on his personal growth at Euclid, Dale observed that his preaching was sharpened. He found more time for reading and reflec-

Dale receives an honorary doctor of divinity degree from Bethany College, 1946

tion, and the articles he wrote for the Euclid *Church Life* were more theologically substantive, more carefully crafted, and more thoughtful than those he had written for the newsletters in his earlier pastorates. The same can be said of his sermons, regularly summarized in his articles. Euclid provided Dale the encouragement, environment, and resources to achieve new levels of writing, thinking, and preaching. Dale recalled some of the influential sources on his thinking at this time—Harry Emerson Fosdick's *Prayer and Guide for Understanding the Bible,* along with Richard Niebuhr's *Social Sources of Denominationalism.*[61]

His leadership skills were increasingly recognized throughout what was still identified as the brotherhood. Evidence of the high regard for Dale's leadership is found in his election as president of the Cleveland Church Federation, chair of the board of directors of the Student Christian Union of Cleveland, trustee of Doctors' Hospital, branch director of the Cleveland YMCA, chair of the Ohio Christian Education Commission 1947–1949, chair of the program committee for the International Convention 1950, trustee of Bethany College 1946, member of the board of managers of the Ohio Christian Missionary Society 1949–1950, and his election to the board of directors of the United Christian Missionary Society in 1946 where he became chair of the board in 1950.

Harry B. McCormick, president of the UCMS, was planning to retire from the office in 1951, one year early. A search was launched for his successor, and Dale was called to become president. About the same time he was offered the chair of homiletics at the Butler School of Religion. Recalling these invitations Dale noted he turned down the offer from Butler because "he was not an academician and had sense enough to know it." But the invitation from the UCMS, he remembered, "sent me to ground zero in re-evaluating my faith. If there had been any doubt I would have said no. It was one thing to mess up a congregation, but quite another to mess up the UCMS. It was a very difficult decision." Ultimately he accepted the call. Hallie Gantz, chair of the search committee, brought Dale's nomination to the UCMS board where it was unanimously approved.[62]

On June 29, 1951, Dale announced his resignation to the congregation. He said simply, "It is with deepest regret that I tender my resignation as pastor of the Euclid Avenue Christian Church, to take effect September 1, 1951 . . . This resignation has been made necessary by my election to the presidency of the United Christian Missionary Society . . . The six years I have been privileged to spend at Euclid Avenue have been the most challenging and satisfying of my twenty-two years as a minister . . . The love which has been so abundantly bestowed upon my family and me will be through the years a cherished memory." The board of elders responded with obvious regret and clear sincerity.[63]

Dear Mr. Fiers,

We are sure that you know without our telling you the very deep regret we, the Elders of the Euclid Avenue Christian Church, have at the news of your leaving. During the years you have been with us, we have learned to love you and to respect you. You have carried us with outstanding success through a period, which might have been a most trying one after the very long ministry of Dr. Goldner, and we feel that we have made progress in every way under your consecrated and inspiring leadership . . . We rejoice that our pastor has been selected for so great an honor. Your field of service is now literally the world.[64]

CHAPTER FOUR

President of the UCMS 1951–1964

The United Christian Missionary Society

At the age of forty-four years, A. Dale Fiers became the fifth and youngest president of the United Christian Missionary Society, the international missionary and education body of the Disciples of Christ. Installed September 19, 1951, as the head of fifty-eight department secretaries and program directors, he was the leader of an organization unusual and unique among denominations. Measured by number of persons, there were approximately 3,000 men and women whose lives were committed to its service: teachers, evangelists, home mission administrators and pastors, state-area-national directors and secretaries, foreign missionaries, native workers, secretaries, writers, and technicians.[1]

The society contained four divisions. Virgil A. Sly who was assisted by E.K. Higdon, Mae Yoho Ward, and Donald West, chaired the Division of Foreign Missions. It provided support for 221 missionaries, 382 Bible schools, 341 mission schools, fifteen hospitals, twenty-three dispensaries, and ninety-six missionary candidates in training. The Division of Home Missions, chaired by Willard M. Wickizer, with fourteen assistants including Clark Buckner, James Sugioka, James Crain, and John Frye, gave oversight to 135 workers in home missions, eighty home mission pastors, eleven migrant staff workers, and six home missions institutions, including the Yakima Indian Christian Mission, All Peoples Christian

Center in Los Angeles, the Mexican Christian Institute, and the Southern Christian Institute. Under the leadership of George Oliver Taylor, assisted by twenty-three staff including Parker Rossman, Charles Marion Ross, and Genevieve Brown, the Division of Christian Education supported fifty religious education field staff and forty-two missionary education field staff all deployed to the various states. It also supported 337 summer conferences, forty-two student centers, four Bible chairs, and 161 World Fellowship Youth meets. Finally, there was the Division of General Administration responsible for resources, interpretation, men's work, treasury functions, audiovisual services, and general services. Dale, with the able assistance of Jessie Trout, Spencer Austin, Louise Moseley, and Francis Payne, gave leadership to this division as well as to the society as a whole.[2]

The enormous scope and scale of the ministry of UCMS in 1950 included 665,713 medical treatments or patient visits on the foreign mission fields and more than seven thousand members added through baptism. On the home mission field, institutions served thirty-five thousand persons to whom seven-and-one-half tons of medical supplies and clothing were distributed annually. Enrollment in home missions exceeded 820, and membership growth by baptism was over 550. It was further estimated that nearly two hundred forty thousand persons had participated in the religious and missionary education programs offered through the society.[3] UCMS was the major source of educational materials and personnel for Disciples congregations everywhere in the world. The ministry of the UCMS was an impressively distinguished, successful, global enterprise, described by at least one historian as "arguably the most powerful and important factor in the development of Disciples church life in the entire history of the Christian Church (Disciples of Christ)."[4]

Dale's first act was to send a letter of greeting and prayer to the extensive network of workers who served in the name of the society. "Today I begin my work with you as a member of the United Society's official family," he wrote. "I can think of no more inspiring description of the worldwide relationships I am privileged to enter than that of the great New Testament missionary who said, 'We are together in God's Service.'" The letter continued for two pages, noting the monumental labor of building such a far-flung educational and missionary enterprise and the demanding tasks ahead. "I wish it were possible," he continued, "for me to greet each one of you whether in Missions Building, the home field, or in lands abroad. Since that cannot be done, I am doing something even more important—I am beginning this day in that spiritual oneness with you, which our precious faith and the power of prayer make possible:

> Dear God, bless my new comrades. Make me worthy of their confidence and friendship. Bind us together in the exaltation of our Lord Jesus Christ, that in all things he might have preeminence. Deliver us from undue concern about things inconsequential; flood our hearts with the holy vision of thy coming kingdom, and enable us to accomplish thy work. For Jesus' sake, Amen.[5]

Virgil Sly once started to write a comprehensive history of the United Christian Missionary Society but died before he was able to produce the work, and no one since has taken up the massive task. In his surviving brief, five-page introduction Dr. Sly set forth his steadfast belief that the United Christian Missionary Society was the result of "an ecumenical awakening of a people as they increasingly involved themselves in the total cooperative and ecumenical concerns of the whole Protestant movement."[6] In Virgil Sly's view the UCMS manifested the wholeness and oneness of the church and was the institutional expression of the belief that the church was one, the mission was one, and the brotherhood was one. It represented in a concrete way the whole spirit and desire for unity and cooperation.

For Dr Sly, the society was more an expression of the philosophical necessity for unity and cooperation than the practical necessity for economy. He saw the formation of the UCMS as a point in the evolution of individual congregations toward the church universal and ecumenical oneness. Organizing the UCMS was the first tangible expression of this concept, a means for the majority of Disciples congregations to realize their search for unity, their struggle to become a church.

A slightly modified perspective suggested that Disciples had proliferated many agencies, and the competitive efforts necessary for their existence had become, in the eyes of many, non-Christian as well as wasteful in the use of personnel, money, and structure to perpetuate their existence. Frederick W. Burnham, former president of the American Christian Missionary Society and first president of the United Christian Missionary Society, was a proponent of this view, citing eight factors that in his opinion, led to the formation of the UCMS:

1. The multiplicity of appeals that had led in 1906 to the appointment of a calendar committee to reduce the number of special day offerings and the subsequent failure of that committee.
2. Unbecoming competition among agencies.
3. Failure of the attempt to have a delegate convention exercise control over the boards in the years 1912–1917.
4. The successful experience of cooperation in the Men and Millions Movement.
5. Recognition of overlapping in some fields and confusion between some organizations because they were doing the same type of work and conducting it in some cases in the same geographic field.

6. Wasted time by officers because headquarters were located in different cities.

7. The danger of overemphasis on a single type of work in a given congregation, to the neglect of other types of work.

8. Publication of its own magazine by each congregation, limited in circulation and subsidized.[7]

A structure of cooperation, according to Burnham, was needed if the leadership was to address the mission of the church efficiently and exercise effectively its responsibility to the church. Duplication of effort and competition for financial support had to be reduced. Contrary to Virgil Sly, Burnham believed the UCMS had developed more out of practical necessity than out of an ecumenical awakening.

The society was organized, its constitution and bylaws adopted, and its first officers elected at the annual International Convention of Disciples of Christ in Cincinnati, Ohio, on October 20, 1919. It was legally incorporated in June 1920. A published handbook defined its existence as "a voluntary expression of the desire of the Disciples of Christ to cooperate in the preaching of the gospel of Jesus Christ at home and abroad and in teaching his way of life. The Society has no motive or purpose aside from the expressed will of those who cooperate through it and who make it their agent." *Those who cooperate through it* was a key phrase because many congregations chose not to support the new UCMS and remained independent of its work. It represented only those congregations and individuals who cooperated with and supported its ministry.

The society's code of regulations added to the statement of purpose that the UCMS was established so "that a world of Christian *brotherhood* may be realized, and that the unity of God's people may be achieved," a statement much in accord with the perspective of Virgil Sly.[8] The term "brotherhood" came in to wide use at this time, implying the existence of fellowship beyond the congregation; a means of group identity without using the detested word, "denomination." Disciples historians Winfred E. Garrison and Alfred DeGroot noted that this step of free cooperation in a religious body of congregational independence was of the highest importance. It came at a cost, however. As early as 1918, the *Christian Standard* magazine opposed the formation of the UCMS because of perceived autocracy and its refusal to promote the restoration ideal. Nineteenth-century Disciples had believed the church could be united through a restoration of New Testament Christianity. Hence the importance of recognizing immersion alone as an acceptable form of baptism and rejecting high criticism of the Scriptures as a rejection of the literal authority of the Bible. The *Standard,* in 1919, proposed the gathering of a congress for the purpose of opposing the formation of the UCMS, along with the "abuses" and "evil" trends in Disciples agencies (i.e., open membership). This led to the creation of a permanent alternative to the International Convention—the North American Christian Convention—and two years of attacks by the *Standard* upon the UCMS. The price paid for the UCMS cooperative unification was the laying of the foundations of an alternative or counter Disciples structure that developed over the next fifty years and emerged as a separate communion in 1968 following the next attempt at cooperative restructure.

Disciples were a frontier people, a part of the emerging concepts of democracy and independence of the nation that gave them birth. Independence and freedom, flavored with a touch of anarchy, were expressed in attitudes that affected their relationship to one another and to the very concept of "organization." It required a considerable period of time for Disciples to realize that a local congregation was not the fullest expression of "church," not a law unto itself. This break from the iconoclastic position of the early Disciples was gradual but clearly evident in the appearance of the voluntary society concept—districts, evangelistic associations, state societies and associations—and the development of national organizations beginning with the American Christian Missionary Society in 1849. Appearing in the 1870s and 1880s were several national organizations—Christian Woman's Board of Missions–1874, the Foreign Christian Missionary Society–1875, National Benevolent Association of the Christian Church–1886, Board of Ministerial Relief–1895—which attempted to structure the idea of cooperative organization inviting individual congregations, as they saw fit, to support cooperative concerns that were beyond the reach of local congregations.

The history of Christianity from the beginning is one of a struggle and search for unity, cooperation, and ecumenical identity. It was true in the first century as well as the twenty-first century. The Disciples of Christ, arriving late on the scene of Christian history, were and continue to be a part of the total frustration of the church in this struggle and search. They, like so many before them, were unable to free themselves from their time and circumstances and often found division within their own ranks rather than the subordination of special interests to the welfare and will of the whole church.

Disciples leaders participating in national and international ecumenical meetings in the early twentieth century had begun to grasp the necessity for a united effort in at least the practical expression of the church's mission to the world. There was a growing sentiment for some form of unification. As early as 1876, the Richmond general convention of the American Christian Missionary Society proclaimed in a formal resolution its hope for a time "when general cooperation of the congregations shall be secured . . . and . . . resolve all these organizations into one."[9] Planning the 1909 centennial of Thomas Campbell's immortal Declaration and Address produced a general cooperation for four years among all agencies—state, national, and educational—demonstrating the possibility and success of cooperation and unity along with the ability to be accountable. The experience of the Men and Millions Movement, a united promotional endeavor inaugurated in 1913, as well as cooperative efforts during World War II, had again confirmed that tasks could be carried out as a brotherhood. W. R. Warren noted in the *Survey of Service* that for a "religious democracy that breaks into a panic at the mere mention of ecclesiasticism," the brotherhood was beginning to take seriously the fact it could actually do things as a "brotherhood."[10]

The United Christian Missionary Society conceived itself to be a creature of the cooperating congregations, brought into existence by members of those congregations and responsible to them. Published pamphlets stated, "The United Christian Missionary Society belongs to and is constituted by all members of the [congregations]." The United Society recognized the autonomy of the local congregation but also its universality as a part of the Body of Christ. Frederick Burnham was quick to say, "The United Society does not take the work farther away from the people—it brings it nearer." In fact the UCMS was a constituent agency of the international convention, carefully formed around two concepts, freedom and responsibility. It was both a society—which made it free—and a board of missions and education—which made it responsible to the congregations.[11]

Dale was a thorough and competent student of both Disciples history and the United Society's history. Although personally inclined toward Sly's perspective, he found truth in both the philosophical necessity interpretation of Virgil Sly and the practical necessity view of Fredrick Burnham. The UCMS was clearly a product of both influences, and it functioned both as a society and as a board, free to cooperate with other religious bodies in the wider church and to be a bridge between the congregations at home and those overseas, yet accountable to the Disciples congregations through the International Convention. Dale also understood the meaning of the word "united," which referred to the union of the American Christian Missionary Society, the Christian Woman's Board of Missions, and the Foreign Christian Missionary Society to form the United Christian Missionary Society in 1920 when the work of the old boards was committed to the new society. Other boards joined briefly—the board of church extension–1883 (originally, like the board of higher education–1894 and the board of temperance and social welfare, a department of the American Christian Missionary Society), the board of ministerial relief–1895 (later the Pension Fund), and the National Benevolent Association–1899—but soon opted for independent status, the Pension Fund in 1928, NBA in 1933, and BCE in 1934.

The new policy governing foreign missions—"Paternalism to Partnership to Autonomy"—had initially been articulated at the Willingen, Germany, conference in 1951. Virgil Sly attended this conference and was one of the architects of the policy. Dale was quite aware his first order of business at the society would be interpreting this policy to the missionaries in the field and to the church at home. It was much more difficult to interpret at home, he recalled, where the thinking was "our" church, "our" hospital, "our" school—rather than partnership or autonomy. Understanding that the business of the mission field was to go out of business was difficult for the congregations at home. Missionaries, however, found that denominations did not make sense on the mission field where there was a growing sense of "church" rather than "society."[12]

A Trip Around the World

In 1952, the UCMS board of trustees suggested to Dale Fiers that he ought to have a firsthand acquaintance with the work of the society, not only on the home field but on the foreign fields as well. This knowledge would enable him to more fully interpret and give overall direction to the world enterprise. Furthermore, the new Willingen policy needed to be presented and interpreted to the missionaries around the world. Accordingly, he organized a three-month trip to visit mission stations in Africa, India, Thailand, and Japan where he would offer a candid appraisal of the new policy and fully record what he saw and heard.[13] He was the first sitting president of the UCMS to visit the foreign missions. On October 20, 1952, Dale left Indianapolis on the first leg of a journey that would take him around the world. He kept a comprehensive daily journal of his travels and observations, making entries on airplanes, ships, trains, trucks, cars, carts, canoes, and at times in bed. His journal was later published under the title, *This is Missions*.

Dr. Virgil Sly, chair of the Division of Foreign Missions, accompanied him. The two traveled by train to New York City where they met with Charles Ranson, secretary of the International Missionary Council, and with Jesse Bader of the National Council of Churches. Following those sessions, Dale noted in his journal, "Missionary strategy in the world Christian movement is in for a basic reconsideration by the missionary statesmen of our time," a direct reference to the impact of the 1951 Willingen Conference.

Around this time Dale's father suffered a heart attack. After receiving word in New York from his brother-in-law, DeWitt Brown, that the condition of his father was stable and improving, Dale proceeded with the trip leaving October 22 on the *Queen Mary* for Europe. He and Virgil spent much of the voyage discussing future strategies in foreign missions, but Dale wrote often to and about his beloved family whom he always identified as his "loved ones." To his daughter, Barbara, he sent congratulations on achieving the honor roll but noted in response to her letter, it was *Silas Marner* rather than *Silo Marner*; to Alan he advised, "Keep the old courtesy brushed up nice and bright."[14] Later in Africa, accompanied always by loneliness, he sent to his "loved ones" a "Congo River full of love."

Five days later they were in London, still blitz-scarred, where they met with R.F.W. Haywood, general secretary of the Baptist Missionary Society, and visited the offices of Norman Goodall and Eric Mielson of the International Missionary Council. The theme of every meeting was "Keeping the door open for total Protestant cooperation in foreign missions and partnership with the mission churches." Dale recorded in his journal after the New York and London visits to the offices housing several prominent missionary executives, "I was impressed by their unimpressiveness. After all, *Pilgrim's Progress* was written in a prison cell. Great work does not require a plush office."[15]

After speaking to several London congregations Dale and Virgil flew to Geneva where Robert Tobias, the Disciples representative to the World Council of Churches, met them on November 3. In Geneva they visited with one of the world's great Christian leaders, Dr. Wilhelm Adolph Visser't Hooft, general secretary of the World Council, with whom Dale shared in several committee sessions and private meetings and of whom Dale noted, "He has a delightful brogue that puts the tonal flavor of broccoli in everything he says."[16]

Following a brief visit to East Berlin where they studied the results of church relief and rehabilitation programs under the auspices of the Lutheran Gosmer Mission, Dale and Virgil flew on to Leopoldville, Congo. The next day, November 14, they traveled by train to Kimpese where they met with Dr. Glen Tuttle and toured the fifty-building Baptist Medical Evangelical Institute—the major medical training center of Protestantism in Congo at that time. It was supported cooperatively by the UCMS and other mission organizations. In the whole Congo there was only one doctor for every thirty-five thousand persons when Dale visited in 1952.[17]

Within one week, they were in the historic Disciples station at Bolenge on the banks of the Congo River. Disciples' missionaries

Ellsworth Lewis, Paul and Esther Snipes, Patty Sly, Carolyn Watkins, Robin Cobble, and Edgar and Edna Pool greeted Dale and Virgil. At a gathering of Congolese Christians early during the visit at Bolenge, a spokesman, as was the custom, conferred upon Dale a Lonkundo name,

Visiting mission stations on the Congo River, 1952

"Bokemyese," meaning "the one who strengthens the work every-where."[18] It was a highly appropriate name for Dale, and he accepted it with humility and seriousness for the heavy responsibility it implied.

In a subsequent Bolenge session with native church leaders, one raised the question, "When will the things we say begin to have authority in the conduct of the mission?" Other equally pointed questions reflect-ed the growing level of local organizational maturity and independence of thought. Dale recorded that "some of these churches are ready for a larger challenge."[19] Later, when he boarded a plane at Coquilhatville to depart the Congo, Dale reinforced this thought in his journal, "It may be many years before I see Congo again, but I shall never forget the devo-tion and the sacrificial spirit I found there nor the fruits of Christian labor [by these] strong and capable Congolese Christians able to carry on in their own right for Christ and the Church."[20]

Dale visited more primitive mission stations at Wema (where he helped baptize over a hundred new converts), Mondombe (where he wrote home to the UCMS trustees "the young church here is rising to a new sense of responsibility"), Monieka, Lotumbe, and Nkone. Riding in a jeep on Congo roads, he joked, "eliminates all necessity for taking Carter's Little Liver Pills to stir up liver action."[21] He visited leper colonies, schools, medical facilities, and numerous local congregations where he often spoke. Of the leper colonies he noted sadly, "You look into the faces with features destroyed by the dreaded disease. You see babies disfigured by its ravaging effects. Your eyes cannot escape the feet half eaten away and hands without fingers." He wrote of the extensive misery and disease he saw everywhere and of the mass of "suffering humanity crying to be healed." "It is so distressing," he noted, "after you have done all you can do, you have only scratched the surface."

Accompanied by John Ross, Dale and Virgil traveled for several days in a small boat down the Momboyo and Congo rivers to Bolenge for the December 9–19 biennial conference of the Disciples of Christ Congo Mission. From all sections of equatorial Congo the missionaries came—seventy-three persons in all. Here, cooperative policy, program, and mission needs were determined for the ensuing two years. He described how distraught the people from Bosobile became when they were informed resources were not available to send a missionary. Dr. Sly tried his best to interpret the hard realities that lay back of the decision, but they refused to speak with him. When the meeting was over, Dale recorded, "Virgil went to his room, put his head in his arms on the table, and wept."[22] At the end of his Congo visit Dale named four problems confronting the ministry of UCMS in Africa: achieving a balance between evangelistic and educational work, determining the extent to which local institutional development should occur, development of national leadership, and development of the indigenous church so it could grow in its capacity to support itself.[23]

Virgil Sly did not accompany Dale on the rest of his travels. Alone with his thoughts on the plane from the Congo to Cairo, Dale reflected on some of the ecclesiastical barriers that prevent congregations as well as religious bodies from cooperating together in world missions. He penned in his journal, "Some of the things that seem so terribly important diminish in significance before the realization of the enormity of the world's need for Christ and the compassion of love."[24]

From Cairo Dale flew to the holy city of Jerusalem in the newly organized state of Israel to visit nearby Arab refugee camps and an Arab orphanage. Of Jerusalem he declared that his most vivid impression was not "of holy places—but of the unholy problems of the contemporary situation," commentary that could just as easily have been written in 2002 as it was in 1952—fifty years earlier. "Jerusalem," he said, "is a city of tensions, war, and strife suspended over its head like the sword of Damocles." The people, he observed, were in a militant mood with little hope of a peaceful settlement. He went on with his commentary to say, "America is becoming increasingly an object of hatred in the Arab world—a people [carrying the] deep hurt and disillusionment of a person who believes he has been betrayed by a friend. The Arabs believe that America's hand is turned against them and that America not only doesn't know the actual situation but is not much interested."[25]

Deeply affected by what he saw and heard, Dale made a special trip to the little garden that surrounds the area of the empty tomb, close by the place of the skull. There he sat down alone and fell into a deep private meditation. He wrote movingly in his journal, "Somewhere nearby the risen Christ said to Mary, 'Peace be unto you.' Here, hope, crushed to the ground, rose again. Is there any hope today? In this last month and a half I have looked upon the stark tragedy of our times. I have seen the children of men bruised, beaten, and left destitute along the highways of life. I have heard from their own lips the despair that floods their hearts. I have smelled the foul air of their refugee camps and heard the cries of little children. I have heard the Christians caught in the vise of events in this city say, 'There is no hope for us here.' . . . Is this the twilight hour of human hope? Here at the empty tomb I reaffirm my own hope and rededicate my own life to the realization of hope through the power of God. It is a hope based not on the might of the kingdoms of this world, but upon the invincibility of the love, truth, and justice which Christ revealed and made the touchstone of man's relationship with man."[26] A deep personal spirituality breathes through these words, words from his innermost being. In them is a universal love and strength of faith that are a conspicuous, enduring, and essential part of him.

From Jerusalem Dale traveled eastward to visit the UCMS mission stations in India, a country living in new independence. On the flight from Karachi to Delhi he had the good fortune to meet the world famous Dr. Frank Laubach with whom he entered lengthy discussion about

Laubach's widely known literacy program, "Each One Teach One," and the way it was assisting the government of India. In Delhi he met Kenneth Potee, secretary of the India Mission, who accompanied Dale to the station at the rural village of Damoh where he saw the hospital, school, and church and met the mission evangelist Peter Solomon, a graduate of Phillips University.

Dale continued by train to the larger mission at Jubbulpore. He was assigned an upper berth with his luggage, while three others in the same compartment were asleep and snoring loudly. Listening to the sounds Dale laughingly supposed one was snoring in Hindi, another in ancient Sanskrit, the other in Arabic, and that he was preparing to make a contribution to the quartet with his own basso-profundo snore with its Indiana twang. Awaiting him in Jubbulpore were a large number of Christmas cards from the members of his former congregation in Newark, Ohio. It was a touching and deeply appreciated surprise. Discussions there focused on the cooperative arrangement with the Baptist Missionary Society. At Jubbulpore he visited the Leonard Theological Seminary, a cooperative enterprise with the Methodist Church, and also toured the 450-student Christian high school, the local church, and a sanatorium.[27]

His itinerary in India included visits to Jyotipur, Kotah, Bilaspur (where he witnessed an eye operation in the mission hospital), Mungeli (where he dedicated a new chapel), and Pendora Road (where he spent Christmas). On Christmas Day in Pendora Road, Dale found himself meditating on the meaning of Christmas, which he expressed in his journal, "Thank God that Christmas in its true meaning is a thing of the spirit . . . a will to peace on earth."[28] Regarding the mission enterprise in India he made reference to a greater receptivity to Christianity now than before independence; an increasing maturity of the church—Indians will be given greater leadership; in the face of rising nationalism, emphasize the transfer of property, responsibility, and program to national hands, and strategically decrease the investment of money and personnel from the outside. Dale thought that the church had about five years left in which to work effectively in India.[29]

Don McGavran was Dale's host in Fosterpur, introducing him to the various projects and showing off a new chapel in a nearby village. Of the jeep ride to the village over oxcart routes and footpaths, with Don driving, Dale noted, "It smacked of the eschatological—last things!"[30] The whole mission, he said, speaks with awe about riding with Don. Dale proceeded to the great agricultural Institute at Allahabad, another UCMS cooperative project, and then to Lucknow for the meeting of the central committee of the World Council of Churches at Isabella Thoburn College—a pillar of the Christian education program in India. Prime Minister Nehru attended the gathering, the first such meeting of the committee in Asia, a deliberate choice designed to recognize the emerging church there. Sir Raj Maharaj Singh, an eminent Indian leader, brought the subject of the place of the missionary in Asia before the assembly. He announced, "The past relationship of missionaries must now change. They must come as partners to share with us."[31] Dale said the comments by Singh touched off a debate that would have far-reaching effects.

A brief three-day stop in Thailand allowed Dale to visit the Nakom Pathom mission near Bangkok. Here the UCMS was in cooperation with the Presbyterian Church in the development of schools (sixteen hundred students attending) and a hospital. Dr. C. Stanley Smith was the host, and their discussion was directed toward the absence of a university to produce leadership for the local church. Here Dale met Disciples missionaries Edna Gish, Ernest Fogg, and Dr. and Mrs. Percy Clark.

The final stop on his global journey was Japan. Anxious to be home with his "loved ones," he wrote a letter to his beloved Betty on her birthday, January 15, as he flew over Formosa.

"F is for the full measure of my love for the sweetest girl in the whole
world.

O is for all things I ought to do for her.

R is for the rough times we have shared.

M is for the motherly way she cares for our children.

O is for the only girl I adore.

S is for the sweetness of her disposition.

A is for the anxiety I have felt during all these days being away.

Put them all together and they spell FORMOSA over which we
have just flown. This is to prove that everything I see now reminds me of
my darling and that I am wishing her all the best on this her Bura Din—
Big Day."[32]

In Tokyo, Dale moderated a gathering of Disciples of Christ pastors
at the Sei Gakuin School. The subject was the cooperative effort with the
United Church of Christ known as Kyodan. Later, Dale visited the grave
of the beloved pioneer Disciples missionary, Charles Garst. His journey
ended with the most memorable visit of the entire trip—the home of his
missionary idol, Dr. Toyohiko Kagawa. During the time they shared
together in his home Kagawa made the statement that would be so influential on Dale's perception of the missionary enterprise. Kagawa said, "If
a church is doing its job in all times and in all places it is involved in direct
evangelism [making Disciples of all nations], educational evangelism
[teaching humankind to observe all things he has commanded], industrial
evangelism [providing food, clothing, and shelter to all people], and
service evangelism [ministering to people in whatever condition]." In
Dale's view, Kagawa was the world's greatest living exponent of this kind
of Christian witness. His work with outcasts, in particular, ranked his
deeds, in Dale's mind, with the work of St. Francis of Assisi for humble
service. The statement made by Kagawa would become a polar star guiding Dale's thinking about the nature of missions.[33]

Two trends were abundantly obvious to Dale during his world tour: the growing independence of the native churches and the success of cooperative efforts with other religious bodies. Stability in the field was found in the places where cooperation was strong, while independent efforts were eternally teetering on the edge of extinction. Where leadership had been properly nurtured the local church was asserting its strength in decision-making roles to set direction for themselves. These important observations informed Dale's own leadership and shaped his decision-making for nearly two decades.

Signs of a new local reorientation, called by some a revolution or transformation, within the missionary enterprise became increasingly evident to Dale. Five years later he was writing of what he called a "revolution" in missions for the publication, *World Call*. Historically, he said, the great emphasis in missions had been the salvation of souls and service to humanity. Consideration of the church as an organization had been secondary. But in the world of the 1950s, strong anti-Christian forces were gaining influence. No matter how strong the schools, hospitals, and other institutions, the church had to be the central bulwark. Although the character of other institutions could be changed and their Christian witness lost to these new anti-Christian forces, the church, despite persecution, was still the church. The "planting and development of mission churches [must] assume a place of prime importance in the missionary enterprise . . . this will determine the missionary strategy of our time and inspire the new directions we take in world mission."[34] Dale voiced his firm conviction "that the missionary obligation rests upon the church on the mission field as well as at home. Indeed, there may be vast areas where *only* the representatives from mission churches will be able to go with the gospel message."[35] Then he stressed, "Mission churches and the institutions associated with them must be helped to move as rapidly as possible from mission direction and support to self-direction and support."[36]

The missionary enterprise was moving inexorably from the stage of paternalism to the new stage of partnership and beyond as had been projected in 1951 when Dale became president of the UCMS. When Dale and Virgil met with the governor of the Belgian Congo during the 1952 tour, the governor proclaimed it would be at least thirty years before the Congo achieved home rule. Independence, of course, came to the Congo in 1960 barely eight years after the governor's pronouncement. The calculations of Dale and Virgil regarding the time to achieve partnership with the local mission churches also missed the mark. Dale observed years later that the mission churches in the Congo were much nearer autonomy than either he or Virgil realized during their visit. The transition occurred in less than twenty years. When Dale visited Bolenge in 1952 he was met by a delegation of Disciples missionaries. When he and Betty returned in 1972 they were met by a delegation of native Christians led by Bishop Bokeleale Itofo Bokambanza.

Dale also discovered that he had to be a constant advocate for the cooperative stance of the UCMS. There were two approaches to missionary work at that time. One was cooperative, a method by which congregations worked together through a missionary society or board and that society or board could then work ecumenically with other religious bodies in the mission field. The other method was called independent, a method of direct support by individual congregations to individual missionaries. Dale believed UCMS to be an expression of the will of the congregations to work with each other in a world program of Christian education, home missions, and foreign missions. He was regularly called upon to defend the cooperative approach, an approach he found in keeping with the spirit and teachings of the New Testament; an approach he was convinced gave stability and continuity to the work of the church in its missionary outreach; an approach that maintained high standards of training and selection of missionaries; an approach of good stewardship that required low overhead costs and conserved the resources of the congregations; and an approach that allowed ecumenical collaboration but was democratic and provided representative management by the congregations who supported the effort.

It was Dale's opinion that Disciples could do comparatively little in the missionary field of the world, at home or abroad, without cooperation. Furthermore, cooperation was an approach in keeping with Disciples history. Alexander Campbell had written in 1842, "We can do comparatively nothing in distributing the Bible abroad without cooperation; we can do comparatively but little in the great missionary field of the world, either at home or abroad, without cooperation; we can do little or nothing to improve and elevate the Christian ministry without cooperation; and we can have no thorough cooperation without a more ample extensive and thorough church organization." No missionary, no mission field, Dale often said, depended completely upon the support of just a few congregations that may or may not continue their interest. This was affirmed by one African missionary who wrote, "We have observed that wherever the United Society has a relationship the work becomes stabilized."[37]

The UCMS at Home

Back in Indianapolis Dale's personal commitment to his work took on a burning intensity. Administrative matters were filled with new significance, and he thought often of "the great service being rendered, the grim problems being faced, the great opportunities that awaited a courageous church." Even the budget was viewed differently. Writing in the June 1953 issue of *Minister's Bulletin,* Dale expressed the passion he so keenly felt. "It is one thing to build a budget in Indianapolis; it is another thing to sit down with missionaries and talk with them about what the budget means. . . . I tell you when you sit down with these devoted ambassadors of Christ at Mondombe . . . the budget takes on flesh and bones and life. When you go to Lotumbe and talk about the leper colony and its ministry to two hundred lepers on the border of life and death who receive help depending upon available resources, then a budget becomes a matter of crucial importance."[38] Clearly, there was a new urgency in his appeal for resources and a new zeal in his interpretation of foreign missions.

Dale's first report of his overseas mission tour experience was an address to the United Society's board of trustees in its Indianapolis meeting, January 27, 1953, less than a week after his return. Then on February 1, he was in Newark, Ohio, sharing the highlights of his trip with the women's group of the Christian Church—and thanking them for their Christmas cards. He wrote several articles on the subject of his tour, delivered numerous addresses, and published a book-length account entitled, *This is Missions.*

The structure of the society itself, Dale learned, needed periodic reform and renewal. The structure had been revised several times since its founding in 1920. In 1956, following one and a half years of planning, a significant reorganization regrouped the four major divisions into three. This adjustment was undertaken to serve the congregations and state societies more effectively. Stimulated by the capital campaign, Crusade for a Christian World (1946–1950), greater coordination of national planning was needed and working closely with the new state coordinating committees had become an imperative. In addition, the growing involvement of Disciples representatives in interdenominational work, such as the new National Council of Churches of Christ, placed increasing demands on UCMS personnel. The major change was the consolidation of the division of home missions and the division of Christian education into the division of home missions and Christian education. One year later it was renamed the division of church life and work. By all accounts the new structure was much more efficient and the transition smooth.[39]

The place of women in the church was always a priority with Dale, a direct inheritance from his ordained mother, Leah. Gertrude Dimke, executive assistant to Dr. Gaines Cook during those years, recalled that Dale always "took a strong stand in support of minorities and of women even though it was unpopular with the general public and with many members of the church."[40] Dale commented openly and frequently on the subject in public addresses and in print: "The service and status of women in the church," he said, "is one of the most important concerns we face in our world. This is not merely a matter of women's rights, but much more basically of the 'wholeness of the church' in its life, work and witness."[41] The ideal of the equality of women in the United Society was incorporated into the formal organizational pattern due to the incorporation of the Christian Woman's Board of Missions when the society was born. Dale took great pride in sharing the ratios of women to men within the structure and ministry of the United Society, which appeared as follows in 1956.

WOMEN	POSITION	MEN
60	Board of Managers	60
11	Board of Trustees	11
4	General Officers	4
3	Executive Secretaries	12
1	Assistant Secretaries	4
15	Directors of National Program	21
11	Departmental Associates	0
6	Service Department Supervisors	6
39	Field Staff: Religious Education	42
148	Foreign Missionary Staff	92
95	Home Missionary Staff	99
393	Total	347[42]

These statistics revealed that women held an equitable place in the life of the UCMS, particularly at the highest levels. One imbalance was the number of executive secretaries; another was that a man had always held the presidency. Overall the leadership of women was recognized more equitably in the UCMS in 1956 than in almost any other religious body in the country and certainly in the social institutions of America at large. Maintaining a balance of the sexes was incorporated into the constitution and code of regulations of the society, making all offices "open to men and women alike . . . [and] it shall be the duty of the president of the Society to call immediately the attention of the Board of Trustees to any unbalance in the representation of men and women. . ."[43]

The recurring subject of open membership, one of the last vestiges of restorationism, occupied a good bit of Dale's thought and attention. The issue had plagued the early years of UCMS history, stunting the development of its rationale for mission. Letters and questions continued to arrive regularly at the society during Dale's years, asking about the attitude of the UCMS toward open membership on the mission field: Were missionaries permitted to receive the unimmersed into full fellowship? Did missionaries have the right to preach anything they desired? Dale, a veteran of open membership tensions at Euclid Avenue in Cleveland, tackled the issue head-on by writing a public response in *Leaven* for the whole church to read: "The attitude toward open membership on the foreign field is exactly the same as the attitude of the Society toward open membership at home, namely, that the right of decision in the matter of determining policies on receiving members is the right of the local congregation. The United Society does not presume to be an ecclesiastical authority making decisions for the local church at home. Neither does it make decisions for mature and self-directing churches on the mission fields. . . . The United Society does not advocate open membership. It is likewise true that the United Society does not break fellowship with those churches either in the homeland or abroad, which by their own decision receive the unimmersed into their fellowship. . . . We will not break fellowship with churches on the basis of that decision."[44]

In regard to the missionaries, Dale stated plainly that the United Society did not require them to sign a creed or statement of faith. They were responsible representatives of the brotherhood and the society, selected because of their commitment. As a matter of fact, he added, "the missionaries are rarely pastors of churches and therefore, are not the ones who receive into membership those who make the confession of their faith." Missionaries were engineers, doctors, and educators, each ministering in different ways. He tried to help his readers understand that when churches organically merge in a given country or area, they become part of a larger fellowship and must contribute their own distinctive witness to the Christian faith. Far from abandoning Disciples principles, he argued, the missionaries provide a Disciples witness that enriches the other churches in the fellowship. Christian unity, he declared, was on the march around the world, and Disciples needed to rise to the challenge and accept their part in the coming together of the church. "Any who reject such cooperation," he wrote, "must follow the logic of their decisions to the point where they give a separate witness outside of all cooperative channels of fellowship with other religious bodies. The United Society is not prepared to take this isolated approach in a time that demands the unity of the church."[45]

Dale and his UCMS team developed a new strategy of world mission in 1959. It stressed two major themes, cooperation and partnership with the emerging national churches. The seven-part plan included, "Worldwide fellowship, with every church becoming a missionary community; United Society seeking always to make the gospel relevant to all people through the rapid social change on the mission fields; older and

younger churches working in partnership to strengthen and enlarge overseas churches; mission and unity by which the United Society participates
in every approved cooperative enterprise to the extent possible; mobility
and flexibility of program; mission and evangelism; and administration that
is shared by representatives of the United Society with the developing
leadership of the emerging national churches."[46] This policy guided the
work of the UCMS during the remaining nine years of its existence.

During these years Dale's ministry began to extend to American
Protestantism, and the global operations of his work took him and Betty
to many countries of the world. He was elected to membership on the
general board of the National Council of Churches and served as chairman of its review of reports committee, which made recommendations
to the general assembly for action. He was a member of the general
program, field and planning committee and also served as chairman of
the North American committee of the World Council of Christian
Education and Sunday School Association. In 1958 he attended the
Tokyo convention of WCCESSA and was a delegate to the 1960 convention in Germany and the 1962 assembly in Belfast, Ireland. In August
of 1956 Dale and Betty represented the brotherhood as fraternal delegates
to the annual conference of the British Churches of Christ in
Manchester, England. Early in 1959 he made an administrative tour of
Caribbean and South American missions and in February 1961 Dale and
Betty traveled to Aguascalientes, Mexico, where he participated in the
laying of a cornerstone for Hope Hospital, a $64,000 structure financed
with Capital for Kingdom building funds. Later that year, in November,
they attended the third assembly of the World Council of Churches in
New Delhi, India, and continued from there on a tour of mission stations
in India, Nepal, Thailand, the Philippines, and Japan.

Four events of 1960 shaped the Disciples agenda for the decade and
beyond and provided the basic content of Dale's ministry for the

remainder of his career. In January of that year a committee of the International Convention recommended the appointment of a commission on restructure of the brotherhood. In February four black students in Greensboro, North Carolina, sat down at a white-only lunch counter, thereby launching a new chapter in the civil rights struggle in America. In June the Belgian Congo received its independence and became known as Zaire. And in December Presbyterian minister Eugene Carson Blake delivered a sermon in San Francisco containing a dynamic proposal for Christian unity that resulted in the formation of the nine-denomination Consultation on Church Union. Dale's report to the board of directors in 1960 marked the fortieth anniversary of the United Christian Missionary Society. Although he recounted its distinguished history the focus of his remarks was on the exploding situation in the Congo and possible consequences—the emerging discussion of restructure and the steps that needed to be taken by the United Society; and the United Society's blueprint for the Decade of Decision in the 1960s, a program of advancement in Christian education, evangelism, and stewardship.[47]

A considerable portion of Dale and Betty's time during the sixties was given to an unexpected issue on the home front—the civil rights movement. The pivotal year was 1963. In April, nonviolent demonstrations designed to integrate Birmingham, Alabama, resulted in the imprisonment of Martin Luther King Jr. and his writing of the class "Letter from a Birmingham Jail," a stirring defense of the nonviolent strategy. The following June television screens across the nation carried the image of Governor George Wallace standing in the doorway of a building at the University of Alabama to block the enrollment of black students. He stepped aside when President John F. Kennedy dispatched Federal marshals to the scene. That evening the president addressed the nation in burning rhetoric, calling civil rights "a moral issue as old as the Scriptures and as clear as the American Constituion,"[48] and he added,

If an American, because his skin is dark, cannot eat lunch in a restaurant open to the public, if he cannot send his children to the best public school available, if he cannot vote for the public officials who represent him, if, in short, he cannot enjoy the full and free life which all of us want, then who among us would be content to have the color of his skin changed and stand in his place? Who among us would then be content with the counsels of patience and delay?[49]

Later that same night, NAACP official Medgar Evers was murdered as he returned to his home in Jackson, Mississippi.

President Kennedy placed before Congress a civil rights bill designed to protect black voters, desegregate the public schools, and end discrimination in public facilities. On August 28, more than two hundred thousand blacks and whites marched on Washington, the largest civil rights demonstration in American history. Standing in front of the Lincoln Memorial, King delivered his famous "I Have a Dream" speech. Two weeks later, Sunday, September 15, a bomb exploded in a Birmingham Baptist church, killing four adolescent black girls. The country was outraged, as were other nations around the globe. There was clearly a moral crisis in the nation over the issues of human rights and social justice. The United Christian Missionary Society was the first to lead on behalf of Disciples during that time of tragedy and protest.

Early in that fateful year the National Council of Churches issued a report to all denominations pointing to the mounting tide of actions that had moved the civil rights issue to the center of the nation's attention. The report called it a moral crisis involving the fundamental concepts of freedom and justice, the concept of common humanity, and the integrity of the church with its faith. Up to this time, the report claimed, it had been possible to rely upon gradual change. Modest progress in racial justice was accepted as the best the church could do. But now the issue was sharply drawn in nearly every corner of the nation. The report, therefore, called upon the church to put aside its "lesser engagement," to confess her own sins of omission and delay, and to witness to her belief that every human being is a child of God. Every member communion of the National Council was urged to impress upon its people the serious nature of the issue and to press vigorously for involvement. The board of the National Council proposed an interdenominational and interfaith approach to the crisis and issued a call for action—even costly action— to take risks, encourage the mobilization of resources, negotiations, demonstrations, and direct action.[50] J. Irwin Miller, president of the National Council and a prominent Disciples layman, stated forthrightly that "racial discrimination violates Christian love and is man's denial of God's rule." He asked the church to pray that racism be eliminated from both heart and practice.

On June 19, Gaines M. Cook, executive secretary of the international convention of Christian churches, wrote a letter to all member agencies expressing full support of the National Council report. Furthermore, the administrative committee of the International Convention had authorized Cook to issue a call to all agencies, boards, and institutions related to the Disciples of Christ to take immediate action to provide the leadership and financial resources necessary to implement a program of negotiations and direct action on the civil rights question. And the international convention quickly established a coordinating committee for moral and civil rights.[51]

The UCMS had acted the day before. Dale, a leader in both the national council and International Convention, led the UCMS to decisive action. The meeting of the UCMS board on that date noted the twenty-six years of resolutions from the annual assemblies of the International Convention condemning segregation and discrimination. Those assemblies had proclaimed, "There is an imperative in the gospel that there be no segregation or discrimination on the basis of color." One assembly had pointed out, "One of the ugly facts of our day is that fellowship of the church is denied . . . by discrimination . . . based upon color." The convention had insisted, "Voting restrictions based on color should be removed." It had also insisted, "As Christians . . . we should remove every barrier that prevents, on the basis of color, any [person] from serving God." It had urged members when they had property to sell to do so without racial restrictions. And these resolutions were made known in every area of church life. Painfully conscious of the inadequacy of Disciples accomplishments, the board confessed, "We have not matched words with deeds."[52]

Among its emergency actions the UCMS Board established its own emergency coordinating committee for moral and civil rights, committed itself to becoming thoroughly involved in the crisis, and urged Disciples and their agencies to coordinate resources and efforts expediently. Dale and his administrative team took direct responsibility for the development of intensified programs in the area of civil rights within the scope of the United Society's responsibilities. The board authorized Dale to set up a special emergency fund of $50,000 out of the fixed reserves for emergency financing. The funds were authorized because the civil rights crisis was considered an extreme emergency. But they were authorized as a loan and with the caveat the funds be replaced as soon as possible from promotional sources.[53] The society then created a set of principles regarding staff involvement in demonstrations: each person could decide to participate or not to participate in demonstrations; nonviolent demonstrations were declared to be in the American tradition of freedom of speech and freedom of peaceful assembly; nonviolent direct action techniques were to be used only after extensive negotiations had been tried without success; in local situations the attempt should always be made to work through local congregations representing both majority and minority involved; the purpose of the Christian's involvement in demonstrations . . . was to bring about justice and reconciliation.[54]

Dale immediately involved himself beyond coordination by participating in the sympathy march in Clarksdale, Mississippi, where a drugstore had been bombed. Martin Luther King Jr. led the march. When Medgar Evers was murdered, Dale was part of the sympathy march in Jackson, Mississippi, and again participated in the first Selma, Alabama, march—King led both marches. Later, in 1968, Dale participated in the Memphis march following the murder of King and in the Poor Peoples March on Washington. In each of these instances, Dale met with local ministers of all faiths to lend pastoral assistance in managing the local challenges to their congregations and to themselves. Betty, too, was actively engaged with the civil rights question. She was well known in Indianapolis and Indiana for her work as president of the United Fund League, board member of the eastside YMCA, president of the PTA, and residential chair of the Marion County United Fund campaign. In 1960 the governor of Indiana appointed her to the state's civil rights commission. She served two terms of four years each. During an attempt to integrate a city park in Indianapolis, burning crosses were placed on the lawn of the Fiers home and the lawn of the governor's mansion. An additional challenge came in 1966 when Disciples leadership in Dallas attempted to prevent Dale from bringing Martin Luther King Jr. to speak at the International Convention, which was to be held in that city. Dale was told, "King is not coming to Dallas!" Dale responded to the local planning leadership that if King was not coming to Dallas, neither was the International Convention. Ultimately a compromise was struck that called for a panel on which King would sit as one of four members.[55] In spite of these and other challenges, Dale and Betty remained fixed in their commitment to social justice.

Dale Fiers with Martin Luther King Jr. (far right) at the 1966
International Convention in Dallas

Meanwhile, the International Convention's coordinating committee on moral and civil rights, chaired by Barton Hunter, also helped with the civil rights struggle. The surviving minutes of their five meetings during the summer of 1963 indicate the committee's authority was constrained by the extent to which agencies, state societies, congregations, and individuals supported it. The committee, born in a burst of compassion and enthusiasm, was initially quite active, sending a letter to all ministers and state secretaries announcing its creation and calling for commitment and cooperation. It also assigned Ian McCrae the task of developing a study pamphlet for use in all congregations and arranged for a shipment of food and clothing to be sent to locations in the Mississippi Delta. It discussed setting up pilot housing projects in selected communities, convening local bankers and real estate brokers to discuss housing and financial assistance for minorities, developing projects for voter registration, and numerous other possible initiatives. In addition, the committee also prepared a proposal to finance their work, namely approval from the convention for an emergency congregational offering of $300,000, to be planned and administered by James Suggs and Spencer Austin.[56]

By its third meeting the committee was enlarged to include state secretaries and agency heads. Its work was soon slowed by questions of polity, a circumstance that can so often lead to moral paralysis. The agency heads wanted the committee enlarged to include a representative from each agency, and they also suggested each agency consider its own course of action. The state secretaries repeatedly emphasized that emergency offerings from congregations had to be cleared through state financial committees and this had not been done. State associations voiced criticism of the coordinating committee, which in their view had acted unilaterally, causing some states and local congregations to withhold funds from Unified Promotion. The states too wanted to follow their own course of action. When state societies were asked about their civil rights programs, they admitted that virtually nothing in the way of program activity existed. Some members demanded rules of procedure for the coordinating committee and a subcommittee was appointed to develop them. It required three meetings to approve the outline of Ian McCrae's pamphlet and then with the understanding it had to be reviewed again before release. When the report on plans for the march on Washington with Martin Luther King Jr. was presented to the committee by George Earle Owen, the majority of those present felt that the goals of the march "went beyond the stated area of concern of the coordinating committee," and the committee, sadly, did not endorse the march. It did say, however, that any individual who cared to participate could do so.[57] In the fifth meeting, October 31, 1963, the treasurer, Howard Dentler, reported eight hundred congregations (ten percent of the reported eight thousand congregations in the brotherhood) had ordered promotional materials on the proposed special offering for civil rights initiatives. The congregations, in the end, contributed a total of $112,000 toward the goal of $300,000.

But the committee produced two very solid achievements. First, it recruited 561 ministers to press for passage of the 1964 Civil Rights Act, wrote thirty-four hundred personal letters to congregations and individuals, and visited members of Congress to urge support for the Civil Rights Act—which passed. Second, the committee helped the church to understand its own shortfall on the issue of civil rights. To the committee's question of "Where are we as a church on interracial personnel at this point?" came the following representative answers for the summer of 1963:

UCMS:
> Blacks employed on both service and national staff;
> Board of trustees and board of managers both integrated;
> Services available to all.

International Convention:
> No blacks employed

National Benevolent Association:
> No blacks on boards
> No adult homes integrated

Board of Higher Education:
> No black employees
> Two blacks on board of directors
> Only Drake University had an integrated faculty
> Four of eighteen colleges still totally segregated

Council on Christian Unity:

> No blacks on staff
>
> No blacks on board of directors

World Call:

> No blacks on staff
>
> No blacks on board of directors

Board of Church Extension:

> One black on staff
>
> One black on board of directors
>
> No discrimination in loan policies

Christmount:

> No blacks on board

National City Christian Church:

> No blacks on staff
>
> One black church member[58]

There were no reports from the other agencies or from the state societies, but this group of nine agencies was largely representative of the whole.

The staff report presented to the International Convention coordinating committee on moral and civil rights in March of 1964 stated candidly, "Despite all of the responses to the original 'call,' the Brotherhood is not operating as if moral and civil rights are a top priority item." The report went on to say, "It seems clear that state and national agencies, with a few notable exceptions, have not assumed any major responsibility for modifying their own programs in response to the national emergency in civil rights. Agency programs are being planned and implemented this year along exactly the same lines as any other year.... Moral and civil rights are not being given major attention at state conventions, nor is the work of the coordinating committee being thoroughly reviewed at the International Convention in Detroit." While few state and national agencies gave civil rights top priority, the report indicated that several local pastors and laypersons had done so. They were involved in protest witnessing and organized support for local ordinances affecting civil rights and for the Civil Rights Act. Ten Disciples ministers had served as observers for the National Council during a voter registration drive in Canton, Mississippi.[59]

Meanwhile, the proactive UCMS was being severely criticized. Its department of community life and social service had been the most active part of the whole Disciples participation in the civil rights movement. Dale responded in a special article for the fall issue of *Leaven* in 1963. He grouped the questions into four categories. First was the category of questions dealing with the United Society's appropriation of a $50,000 loan to support the total program of the brotherhood. Some critics claimed it was a misappropriation of funds, an unauthorized use of missionary dollars outside the rightful boundaries of UCMS responsibility. Dale explained the use of funds was wholly proper and clearly within the established frame of responsibility of the society which was to exercise leadership in the field of social witness and service. The money was advanced as a loan, but even if it should not be repaid, said Dale, it was not a misappropriation because the world mission of the church is one and indivisible.[60]

The second area of criticism focused on the participation of society employees in demonstrations. He explained the need to go beyond resolutions and words in ways that would witness to the Christian faith. Direct action, he said, was suggested in the framework of nonviolence and guided by the spirit and intent of the resolutions passed almost unanimously in the convention assemblies for more than a quarter of a century. "I myself have engaged in direct action. At no point have I found myself identified with mob action, plotting violence, or doing anything other than making a positive Christian witness . . . The right of peaceful protest is the essence of our democratic way of life."[61]

The third area of criticism suggested that the real intention of the leaders was to divide and disrupt the church in America. Dale replied that this was simply not true. "The real intent," he wrote, "[was to make] the churches obedient to the gospel if it is to become a redemptive and reconciling force in the present, revolutionary situation . . . There was a dramatic realization that the church was facing a clear-cut moral issue in regard to racial segregation. It was recognized to be a matter of right and wrong."[62]

Finally, there were the criticisms about procedure. Some believed the actions of the society represented an unwarranted usurpation of authority without proper clearance. Action, they suggested, should have been postponed until the Miami assembly in the late fall of 1963. Dale assured the critics that every form of clearance under existing structures had been carefully observed. Then he concluded, "Conceivably, action could have been postponed until the Miami assembly, but if this had been done our brotherhood would not have played a redemptive part in the crucial developments of this summer. Its voice would have been an inaudible whisper in the long, difficult period ahead of us when the church's voice of concern, love, and reconciliation will so desperately need to be heard."[63]

In the spring of 1964, at an Indianapolis Lutheran church, Dale preached one of his most eloquent sermons on civil rights, "Beyond Words to Achievement." He began by noting there was no lack of words of high idealism in the historic struggle but said we must move beyond words to achievement in our national life through enactment of strong civil rights legislation; move beyond words to achievement in our church life through the desegregation of institutions and practices; and move beyond words to achievement in the desegregation of our own individual hearts. There is a new heart, he proclaimed, a desegregated heart found in more and more individuals as the inner struggle comes to the moment of decision. It was a profound statement. And if anyone ever doubted Dale's dedication to the issue, that person needed only to hear or read this sermon.[64]

On October 1, 1963, Dale was elected executive secretary of the International Convention. The previous year he had been elected executive secretary of the commission on restructure. And he was still president of the United Christian Missionary Society. He would hold all three positions for one year. In his final year as president of the United Society he prepared a digest of criticisms of the society and shared his thinking on their merit. Many criticisms came from the state associations. The conference of state and area secretaries and board chairs, established in 1962, a recent addition to the constellation of organizations, was flexing its new organizational muscle. Among the criticisms were use of money without sufficient consultation with the states; the need to expand state services, failure to consult with state secretaries on the new regional leadership program, improper use of staff in the field with disproportionate time spent in local congregations, efforts that could better be made by the states, duplication of services that could better be rendered b   y state leadership; excessive travel which restricted money for state staff to travel. The addition of staff to the National Men's Work Department was criticized as "wild cat" financing—and state societies asked if they could use the same method. Critics felt that a disproportionate share of resources was going to small states while large states were under severe limitation, and the society's nominating procedures were called nondemocratic [three from Texas, none from Missouri]. Dale commented on the criticisms, "The more unified we become the more basis there is for this kind of criticism within the family. It is a sign of our closeness, not our separateness." He added, "Many of the criticisms might with equal or greater relevance be expressed by the Society with regard to other [agencies]—especially the states." He then concluded that careful study was needed to chart a future course of action in interpretation, consultation, program, and organizational relationships.[65] From the perspective of some, however, it was the growing strength of the states that led to the ultimate breakup of the UCMS.

A few months later, in June of 1964, Dale, as leader of the church, was called upon to testify before the House Judiciary Committee in Washington, DC, on the Becker Amendment, which would have permitted prayer and devotional Bible reading in public schools. Speaking before the committee members he reviewed several recent actions of the Disciples' International Convention on the subject, remarking, "Recent national gatherings of the members of our communion have clearly shown that they are sharply and almost evenly divided on this issue. It seems clear that this is true for the rest of the nation." This is not the time, he advised, for drastic action. Dale then offered a clear and concise statement of his position on the issue. "There are many complex and unanswered questions which must be dealt with before wise solutions to the problems being faced can be achieved. To oversimplify these problems and thus polarize the sentiment of our country by attempting a hasty modification of the Bill of Rights may do irreparable harm to the future of religious freedom and religious faith in our nation. I therefore speak in opposition to the proposals calling for an amendment to the Constitution. I would urge the Congress to lay this matter aside until there has been a more adequate opportunity for national discussion and creative thinking on the ways and means by which this issue can best be resolved." He urged the committee to consider the hearings the beginning of a significant national discussion of the issue rather than the basis for a hasty and perhaps ill-conceived constitutional change.[66]

Dale's final term as president of the UCMS was filled with many memorable family milestones, which gave him a transcendent satisfaction and happy release from the demanding responsibility of the presidency. "The total family was a unit," recalled Gertrude Dimke. "He knew what was going on at home even when traveling."[67] Each summer the family vacationed together, partly in Michigan, partly at West Palm Beach. Barbara completed high school in 1954 and enrolled at Bethany College where she pursued her interest in art. She graduated in 1958 and in June

Leah and George Fiers' fiftieth wedding anniversary; left to right, Bethel, Dale, Leah, George, Othel

married her college sweetheart, Hugh Edward Joyce.

Alan Fiers was an outstanding high school football player during the mid-fifties, and Dale often reorganized his schedule to be present for those games. Alan subsequently attended Ohio State University where he was a first team starter for Woody Hayes and was selected to play in the Blue–Gray game. Dale reveled in those Saturday games. Alan married Hazel Baur in December 1960, another happy family benchmark of those years.

George Fiers, Dale's father, died in 1956, and his mother, Leah, followed in 1962. Then in September of 1962 Barbara gave birth to Hugh Jr., the first grandchild. In June 1963, Alan's daughter Kim was born, and in December of that same year a daughter, Stephanie, was born to Barbara. The birth of those granddaughters was a welcome touch of grace to a period otherwise darkened in Dale's experience with civil rights atrocities and the death of his parents. The circle of "loved ones" grew by two more additions, a daughter, Elizabeth, born to Barbara and Hugh in 1966 and a daughter, Leah, born to Alan and Hazel in 1968. In his installation address given to the international convention in 1964 Dale remarked warmly, "We are just becoming involved in the delights of grandparenthood in our house. One of the expressions I hear with increasing frequency is, 'Oh, we must get that for the children.' What exuberant joy one would miss without the privilege of being a little lavish where the grandchildren are concerned."[68]

Similar to the pattern in his own childhood home, religion did not dominate the lives of Dale's children, but it was clearly integral to their pattern of living. They attended church and church school every Sunday; and they shared in prayer at the evening meal and at bedtime. Attendance at Christmas Eve service was a family tradition, as was Dale's reading of the Nativity story from Luke on Christmas morning. Beyond these selected spiritual disciplines the religious choices of the family members were their own. Church and family received parity in the Fiers household. Reflecting on the role of his parents, Alan Fiers remembered his mother, Betty, as a woman of "steely toughness," both psychologically and intellectually. She was, in Alan's judgment, a steadying influence on his father, whom he described as the more silent of the two, the ameliorator, the more liberal, the one with the softer heart. Together they were a formidable team, sharing a telling influence upon each other and upon the family as a whole.[69]

Dr. Virgil Sly succeeded Dale as president of the United Christian Missionary Society in September of 1964. Dale's accomplishments had been profoundly significant. A partial list containing only twenty-four of those accomplishments was circulated across the whole church, but this list did not convey the true substance of his leadership. Beyond the list—which included the reorganization of the society with several new departments, the transfer of administration and property from the United Society and missionaries to the national churches, helping those new churches become united churches, development of new world mission strategies, activation of the School of Missions, the addition of a new wing to the Missions Building, leadership of the Decade of Decision, the merger of staff and services with the National Christian Missionary Convention, participation in the civil rights movement, and numerous other landmark achievements—was the spiritual strength, integrity, vision, and courage he portrayed and inspired through his own leadership.[70]

Particularly spiritual strength. It was the recognition of this quality that drew people to Dale, that caused them to trust him, that caused them to respect him with such affection as a leader. Evidences of his spiritual strength are found in two small books, *Lord Teach us to Pray,* and *Prayer, and the Great Decisions of Life,* both written by Dale in 1960 and 1961 respectively. "As a young preacher," he wrote, "I once read a book on the life and work of the minister. I have long since forgotten the name of the author and the title, but I remember one sentence—'The unspiritual minister stands unmasked before his people at the time of the pastoral prayer.'" He continued by pointing out when you probe into the realities of spiritual power and confront the power of prayer at work in the world, you can become overwhelmed by your own lack of spiritual depth and poor mastery of the spiritual resources which God has so graciously put at the disposal of his people. It was the growing awareness of the power of prayer in the life of Jesus, he added, that caused his disciples to cry out, "Lord teach us to pray." Then he advised, "I remember Professor Irvin T. Green of Bethany College used to say to young preachers-in-the-making, 'You will find one or two people in every congregation you serve who know God and live close to Him. Be near to these people and learn from them.'"[71]

Dale's life turned on the experience of prayer. Those who have heard him pray never forget the eloquence of his words, how their own hearts were freshly attuned, how perspectives changed and horizons broadened. The moments of pastoral prayer, public invocations, and benedictions were always moments of exceptional strength for Dale, never an unmasking. People recognized both the depth and sincerity of his faith in those prayers and knew instinctively this spiritual strength was the bedrock of his being.

CHAPTER FIVE

The Restructure Dream 1964–1973

Executive Secretary of the International Convention

July 1, 1964, marked a turning point in the life of the Disciples brotherhood and in the life of A. Dale Fiers. On that day he became executive secretary of the International Convention of the Christian Churches (Disciples of Christ), the top executive post among the organizations of the Christian churches. He had been elected to the position at the Miami Beach assembly the previous October, succeeding Dr. Gaines M. Cook who retired after eighteen years as executive secretary. The International Convention—formally organized in 1917 as the International Convention of Disciples of Christ, later changing its name in 1957—wielded no power over the six thousand congregations nor any control over its twenty-one member and affiliated organizations. But for the nearly 1,800,000 Disciples it was the focal point of all they tried to do together. The slogan of the convention was "Building a Brotherhood through Voluntary Cooperation," and its constitutional preamble presented its purpose as "facilitating closer cooperation among the various agencies."[1]

Dale's decision to resign as president of the UCMS, the largest and strongest unit in the church, to become executive secretary of the International Convention, T. J. Liggett remembered, was " a very important decision personally and substantively. It sent a powerful message to

Dale's installation as executive secretary of the International Convention, 1964.

everyone. Dale's leadership provided an incarnation for restructure."[2] Kenneth L. Teegarden attached the same importance to the event, and added, "Dr. Fiers was universally recognized as a spiritual leader who imbued the process with spiritual depth. His enormous personal integrity, strong commitment to Disciples traditions, administrative experience, and pastoral concern made him the single most important person to the success of restructure."[3] And Dr. Joseph Smith added, "I believe restructure really began when Dale Fiers decided to give up the presidency of the United Christian Missionary Society . . . Dale Fiers was Mr. Disciple as president of the United Society and executive secretary of the International Convention and I think that is one reason restructure carried . . . we had a good sense of carryover through Dale, a sense of unity and doing something together under the leadership of this man."[4] No one else could have done what he did. His decision to resign as president of the UCMS in order to accept election as executive secretary of the International Convention was seen as an act of integrity, an ultimate act of commitment to restructure, a bridge of continuity to the new structure, and an act of spiritual discipline growing out of his well-known daily habit of devotions and prayer. Recalling the choice, Dale said it was "a tough decision; a watershed decision for me. My passion was the search for an expression of 'church,' not a group of societies. Yet I loved the United Society, and every time I revisit the moment, I have to justify it all over again."[5]

Dale was to continue as legal head of the UCMS, with Mae Yoho Ward carrying the administrative responsibilities until October 1. The new president would be installed on the second of October, and Dale's formal installation in his new post would occur at the Detroit International Convention on October 4. Marking the transition, Herald B. Monroe, general secretary of the Ohio Society of Christian Churches, wrote a strongly worded article of support. "In a period of uncertainty and change I cannot think of anyone superior to Dale Fiers to whose leadership I would more willingly pledge my support and entrust my church . . . This is not a time for the timid nor the cautious to lead . . . Dale quietly manifest[s] such unintimidated courage that he inspire[s] the rest of us to do what we know our Lord wants us to do. All are aware that when he sees clearly his Christian duty, he will say in a quiet, determined voice, 'We simply must do this!'—regardless of how painful the consequences may be. I am grateful for a leader from whom no timid note is likely to be heard as we move into new times."[6] Such words were a comfort to Dale because he knew the unrelenting criticisms hurled at him during the next few years would cut deep.

His formal installation occurred as scheduled. On that October night in Detroit Dale turned the attention of those gathered to the years ahead, declaring that the Disciples of Christ "cannot stand still. They must progress or regress . . . grow or disappear."[7] His six-part design for progress was an affirmation of faith, rooted first in the Holy Scriptures, second in the great principles of Disciples history, and finally in the astonishing ecumenical advances of the time:

DESIGN FOR PROGRESS

The unceasing pursuit of the Biblical faith and courageous obedience to its high demands.

The development of one common life in the church so faith and spiritual vitality make us worthy to receive, sustain and put to work the new Disciples of this generation.

An increasing measure of liberality and cheerfulness in the management of our lives and resources as God's stewards.

A *relevant church* dealing with Christian solutions to the real issues in our world where moral and spiritual leadership is called for.

The development of structure and order *to manifest the nature of the church* and to carry our share of responsibility for the world mission.

Implicit trust that in all things God is working for good, and that his mercy and grace are sufficient to make our efforts worthwhile . . .

As was his custom, Dale used many references from Scripture and spoke openly and honestly on the key issues facing the church, refusing to skirt controversial questions. He spoke first of the historic vision of Disciples, calling for obedience to the wholeness, unity, and faithfulness of the church in those things, which on divine command, are essential. We have a precious heritage, he said, but "let us be clear what that heritage is and what it is not. It is not uncritical acceptance of the results of the study and work of our pioneers as something final and fixed. It is the faithful and unremitting effort to test all things in terms of the Scriptures under the guidance of the holy spirit . . . We honor the fathers of our movement . . . But it is no mark of honor to them if we cling to viewpoints and understandings which are not Scriptural and theologically valid in the new light which breaks forth from God's word in our day."[8] The recently received advice from the World Council of Churches for denominations to reevaluate their structures in light of the post–World War II world and its culture is evident in Dale's installation address.

Next, he challenged the church to examine its relevance in the struggle for moral and civil rights for all citizens. "The church," he said, "cannot be irrelevant—a faceless, voiceless nonentity on such an important issue. It must speak and live as a relevant factor in bringing reconciliation and influencing the legislative, executive, and legal branches of government to secure human rights for all citizens."[9]

In the fifth part of his design for progress, he set the agenda for his years as executive secretary, knowing that the key issue of his tenure would be restructure. Given the profound leadership role Dale was called upon to provide during those years, it is important to know his perspective on the issue at this crucial juncture in his ministry. Citing the apostle Paul in his first letter to the Corinthians—"In short . . . let all be done decently and in order,"[10] Dale called for a measure of decency and order "in our life as a common people. A clear mandate rests upon us to develop relationships and structures which are compatible with the nature of the church . . . and serve to edify its people and build up the whole body . . .

we are in the youth of life as a people. It is no wonder we feel challenged by the call of this Convention, its associated agencies, and cooperating congregations to engage in comprehensive planning and restructure. The extent to which we are able to re-order our relationships as a people and re-mold our organizational structure in harmony with developing insights into the nature of the church . . . will be one of the major factors of advance and progress."

Then came his trumpet call to restructure: "The ecumenical movement calls us into the unceasing quest for unity of the whole church . . . The Disciples of Christ have made their stand on the conviction that the denominational system . . . falls short of the New Testament concept of decency and order which should characterize the church's life . . . Our search for structure can never be satisfied short of the manifestation of the full unity in the church for which our Lord prayed . . . We can never be content to stumble and crawl into church union out of weakness [or] to live isolated from the church's great struggle for wholeness. We must never . . . let ourselves think we can carry the responsibility for Christ's mission to the world on our own shoulders."[11] His powerful plea for restructure and a theology of "church" was grounded in Scripture, in Disciples history, and in the strong ecumenical currents of that day. And he stood before them as one who had acted on the strength of his own convictions by accepting the office into which he had just been installed.

During this same time, Betty was also installed into an important position of Disciples leadership. On June 30, 1966, she was elected to a four-year term as president of the 237,000-member International Christian Women's Fellowship. In that year there were 4,250 local CWF organizations. As president she presided over the ICWF commission and advisory council, the ICWF gatherings at the International Conventions, as well as the quadrennial assembly. Active as a community leader in Indianapolis, she was also former president of her local CWF at Downey

Avenue Christian Church as well as vice chair of its board of elders. She served as ICWF president while Dale was executive secretary of the international convention and during his early years as general minister and president. Dale and Betty were at the apex of their mutual ministries and worked closely with each other. They were respected as the spiritual, titular, and elected leaders of the Christian Church (Disciples of Christ) in the United States and Canada.[12]

Restructure Background: 1958—1964

A question often raised in different ways during the three decades following restructure was "What prompted restructure?" "What was the reason for restructuring?" "Why did we do it?" Alfred DeGroot once wryly observed, "Disciples were such a variegated brotherhood with such a wide variety of expressions that whatever reason you want to find for restructure, just look and you will find it." In the early 1990s the Disciples of Christ Historical Society conducted oral interviews with forty-seven leaders of restructure, and the first question raised was, "What was the root of restructure." There were five general responses.[13]

First, it was noted in some responses that the World Council of Churches at that time initiated an effort urging all denominations to study their structures in light of post-World War II social changes. They were asked the questions: "Does your structure facilitate the fulfillment of the mission of the church?" "Is the structure of the church responsive to the culture and to the world of the 1950s and 1960s?" Thus, all denominations at that time began evaluating their structures, looking at options, and making some modifications. By this reckoning the Disciples' initiative in restructure did not occur in isolation but was part of a general religious undertaking.[14]

Second, the multiplicity of agencies, both state and national, within the Disciples had resulted in a complex, multilayered system, grown like

Topsy with no real coordination. An agonizing appeal from congregations and the council of agencies demanded that an alternative be found to the freewheeling way of carrying out the mission, some practical means of cooperation. Many organizations had been formed but not much unity. The various agencies and states needed a more integral kind of unity, a more responsible mode of decision making, a way of being held accountable. There was hope for connected relationships among congregations, regions, and agencies, and a hope for some form of representative delegate assembly to engender accountability.[15]

Third, Disciples had matured as a church into something more than a loosely knit collection of congregations with agencies. An inadequate understanding of Church was reflected in an inadequate structure. Essentially, Disciples had no theology of Church beyond the local congregation. Among seminary-educated Disciples clergy there was a growing sophistication, and they understood the nature of Church, what it ought to be, and what it could be. Yet, in spite of the growing conviction that Church was something more than the sum total of local congregations, Disciples did not have a way to speak as Church. There was a hunger for a more "churchly" Church, a hope that the Christian Church could become a reality in the place of just churches, a hope for recognition that the Church exists in regions and in general agencies just as surely as in local congregations.[16]

Fourth, the growing strength of the ecumenical movement caused many to seek restructure as a means of finding an identity, to identify the movement as more than a patchwork of agencies. It was believed this identity was a prerequisite to full participation in the ecumenical movement, its councils, and its cooperative ventures. This feeling grew out of a virtual explosion of ecumenical activity during that period, such as the establishment of the World Council of Churches in 1948, the National Council of Churches in 1950, the Consultation on Church Union in

1960, and Vatican II in 1962. The momentum of ecumenism gave impetus to the Disciples quest for restructure.[17]

And fifth, the United Christian Missionary Society was a powerful Disciples agency, often resented because it was so much larger, had so much more budget, so much more programmatic material, and exercised so much more authority and leadership than the other agencies or states. It was criticized as being too big. Restructure was sought by some, particularly states, to trim back, if not break up, the UCMS.[18]

While each of these forces held its place in the pantheon of Disciples motives for seeking restructure, Dale's unshakable passion was to form an expression of "Church." More than any other person, the vision of church as opposed to some configuration of churches (congregations) in the plural was his. Ronald Osborn had once suggested "Communion of Christian Churches," but Dale would not be moved. The restructure commission once suggested "Association of Christian Churches," but Dale would not settle for anything less than a full understanding of "Church." He believed too that restructure was a continuous process throughout the whole of Disciples history and was in fact a source of renewal. This view was drawn from a lifetime of reading Disciples' history, which left him under its spell. Growing out of his appreciation for Disciples history was his conviction that restructure during the 1960s could not be understood without seeing it against the background of cooperative history and against the background of our peculiar heritage of shifting and contradictory attitudes toward organization, which helped fracture the movement. He also believed that the new structure must belong to Disciples history and therefore should be built of the stuff of history. So Dale always insisted on historical context when he wrote or spoke about the subject.[19] Reflecting on restructure in 1992 and again in 1999, he provided the following summary historical backdrop for restructure on both occasions:

I believe you cannot understand the "Dream of Restructure" without seeing it against the background of history out of which it emerged . . .

Thomas Campbell's declaration that the Church of Christ on earth is essentially, intentionally and constitutionally one is basic. Along with it stands the Last Will and Testament of the Springfield Presbytery. These are reminders that we began as a movement to restore the unity of the Church on the basis of the New Testament. The Christian Association of Washington, Pennsylvania, was organized to promote this plea (but when its message was not getting through as an association they changed from an association to a church, Brush Run Church) . . . There was a great passion for throwing off the trappings of denominationalism with its hireling clergy, man-made organizations, divisions, and creeds . . . and to function out of a strict congregationalism. But our founding fathers also believed that the unity of the Church of Christ on earth was a necessary prerequisite for the successful carrying out of the Church's mission.

As time passed it became apparent that the urgencies of the mission in the world could not wait, and "restored local congregations" were not in and of themselves equipped to do what needed to be done in district, nation or world . . . The watershed event in this period was the calling of a general convention in 1849, which was intended to be a delegated body, but it turned out to be a convention. Its main achievement was the formation of the American Christian Missionary Society to carry out the mission of the congregations at home and abroad. Its creation created a controversy, namely whether organizations beyond the local congregation were Scripturally warranted. The inescapable tension caused by the belief that nothing beyond the local congregation was "Church" brought forth the voluntary society concept, which allowed acceptance of organization in practice but repudiation in principle of ecclesiastical structure. To keep the brotherhood together they decided that any organization beyond the local congregation had to be a society, not of congregations but of individuals. Representatives from local congregations in cities, counties, and even states then began to form societies and boards to undertake mission tasks . . .

By the end of the century the Woman's Board of Missions, the Foreign Christian Missionary Society, Board of Ministerial Relief, Board of Church Extension and Benevolent organizations had been formed, along with various state societies . . . In the midst of this expansion there were attempts at unification, especially in the area of promotion and finances. The Louisville Plan of 1869 was one such failed attempt . . . The plan was to link congregations to districts, districts to states, states to the national with voting representatives from one determining the membership of the other and to have congregations send their missionary offering to the district which would take out enough to support its budget. The rest would be sent to the state to do the same thing and the remainder would go to the national societies to support their work. The problem was, money never got beyond the district.

It was during this period that the seeds of future division were sown by recurring controversies as Disciples tried to define the nature and implications of "the movement." Three distinct currents emerged and were characterized by these names: Non-instrumentalists (Churches of Christ), Independents (Christian Churches and Churches of Christ), and Cooperatives (Christian Churches [Disciples of Christ]). Restructure has its roots mainly with Cooperatives, although the Independent viewpoint had considerable impact upon the process and the outcome.

A number of very significant developments in the first half of the twentieth century affected the "Dream." First, there was an attempt in the 1913 general convention held in Canada to establish a new structure (even more churchly and ecclesiastical than the 1960s restructure) for Disciples that would link general societies and state societies into one structure. It failed. But the compromise that grew out of it was the establishment of the International Convention of Christian Churches at Kansas City in 1917. Second was the creation of the United Christian Missionary Society in 1919-1920, which brought all of the major general societies and boards into one administrative unit. It was the intention that state societies would follow by establishing an administrative linkage with the United Society. Frederick Burnham, president of the society, convened the state secretaries to set the process in motion and that is where it ended. The UCMS failed to unify the raising and distribution of funds, and that brought about Unified Promotion in 1935, an attempt to coordinate promotional and programming efforts.

[Then] an avalanche of interagency cooperation caused us to dream the "Dream." Creation of the Home and State Missions Planning Council-1938; the success of the Emergency Million Campaign to aid stranded missionaries after World War II; the Crusade for a Christian World-1946; creation of the National Church Program Coordinating Council-1950 to plan and execute program together; the Curriculum and Program Council-1953 to develop Christian education materials; and, in the fullness of time, the council of agencies-1950, consisting of every national, state, and educational institution of the Disciples of Christ [It became a focal point for the push toward restructure]. This was an attempt to think, plan, and act with a church-wide perspective. One of the fruitful results was the long-range plan for the 1950s. The impact of all these developments led our communion to think of itself as something more than a disconnected number of independent congregations . . . It was largely out of this flow of events I have tried to summarize that the International Convention meeting in Louisville in 1960 authorized the appointment of a representative Commission on Brotherhood Restructure whose responsibility was to propose a design for the Christian Church."[20]

Most students of restructure point to the year 1958 and the address of Willard Wickizer to the council of agencies meeting in Canton, Missouri, as the fundamental founding moment. Yet, even this pivotal moment was preceded by numerous successful cooperative ventures already noted, along with several ad hoc committees generally appointed by the council of agencies. Among these were the Committee on Brotherhood Organization and Interagency Relationships, chaired by Wilbur Cramblet in 1956, and the Conference on Unification held at Indianapolis in the spring of 1958. But the key event of 1958 was Wickizer's address, which crystallized the need for restructure and spurred the process into action.

Willard M. Wickizer, known as a master organizer, was chair of the UCMS Division of Home Missions. "Wick," with his resemblance to Churchill, self-confidence, ever-present cigar, and stubborn determination, had a reputation for getting things done. He had uttered the oft-quoted statement, "The desire of Disciples to work together and cooperate exceeds their means to do so." Now his colleagues would credit him with igniting the restructure process with his famous address. On that day in Canton,

Wickizer began, "As a brotherhood we have always found it easier to create new coordinating bodies than to actually restructure our organized life and thus eliminate overlapping and competition at its source. At no time in our history, except in very recent days, has anyone dared to suggest that what the Disciples of Christ needs to do is to look at its total organizational structure and attempt a major restructuring that would result in more effective cooperation. Now it would seem that we have reached a degree of maturity as a religious body when such a restructuring might be faced with some hope of success."[21]

But he was adamant that control of congregations was not the goal. "Personally, I feel that if [Disciples] were to get the idea that anybody was seeking to restructure the brotherhood in order to exercise greater control and to limit the autonomy of the local [congregation] the reaction . . . would be violent. We have been strongly congregational from the very first . . . and the vast majority of our people are determined that we shall stay that way."[22] He went on to say "our rather extreme congregationalism probably reflects more the spirit of the frontier on which we were born than it does the teaching of the New Testament."[23]

> We must come to appreciate the fact that freedom carries with it responsibility . . . and that free persons in Christ must cooperate effectively with other free persons in Christ to accomplish these things we cannot do alone. In restructuring the brotherhood we must preserve the principle of voluntarism on the one hand but must magnify the principle of responsibility on the other. That we have had too much of the former in the past and not enough of the latter goes without argument, but we must not be guilty of destroying the one to achieve the other. Responsible discipleship within the framework of freedom, then, should always be our organizational goal.[24]

Wickizer proceeded at length with this theme, stating that Disciples did not need "a more authoritative structure that limits the principles of freedom and voluntarism, but a greater realization of the responsibility that their freedom lays upon them. Too frequently in the past we have wanted to prove our freedom by refusing to cooperate when all the time we could have proven it just as well and far more constructively by cooperating together for the advancement of God's kingdom."[25] He spoke on the strengths and dangers of the newly emerging state organizations, advocating this as a desirable end but expressing hope for some uniformity in pattern. He spoke too of national matters, stating that the International Convention should remain at the heart and all organizations stem from it. He acknowledged the sentiment to make it a delegate assembly and spoke in general terms about other agency reorganization. He concluded, "Of this I am sure, it is high time our brotherhood take a look at its organized life in its totality and restructure it according to a basic plan. For too long we have been willing to add patch on patch, never moving according to a carefully worked out master plan. I believe the mood of our people would support such an undertaking at this time."[26]

Dale was chair of the council of agencies and had given his own address to the Council during that meeting, recounting their nearly ten-year history and noting that in the 1954–1956 biennium the council had turned its attention more definitely to matters of organizational philosophy and structure. As a result the meeting of the council at Bethany College in 1956 made this aspect of the council's work a major emphasis and appointed the Committee on Brotherhood Organization and Inter-Agency Relationships. He prophesied a heavy agenda ahead.[27]

Then came Wickizer's address and the council acted immediately on the restructure agenda. It recommended a Study Committee on Brotherhood Structure be appointed at the International Convention meeting at St. Louis in October 1958. The convention approved a study committee of eleven members and appointed Wickizer as chair. Using a questionnaire the committee consulted thousands, asking what could be done to resolve the inefficiencies within existing structures. Its report to the International Convention at Louisville in 1960 suggested a rationale for restructure, recommending its scope, suggesting listening conferences and lectures along with the recommendation to appoint a commission on restructure. The convention agreed to appoint a commission composed of 120 to 130 persons, to be as representative of all the churches as possible and to have a central committee of fifteen to eighteen members. Granville T. Walker, senior minister of University Christian Church in Fort Worth, Texas, was chosen chair. With "desire, readiness and expectancy for structural change" the recommendation for a commission was enthusiastically approved by the convention and its membership appointed in 1961.[28] The concrete beginnings of restructure were in place, the result of a steady twentieth-century trend of coordination and unification by one group of Disciples known as Cooperatives. An equally steady trend of disaffection gained momentum among another group of Disciples known as Independents. But by 1960 the voluntary society concept had been displaced in the thought of Cooperative Disciples.[29]

The Formation of an Expression of Church: 1964–1968

(Administrative Secretary of the Commission on Brotherhood Restructure)

At the Los Angeles convention in 1962, Dale was appointed administrative secretary of the commission, replacing George Earle Owen who had been on loan from the UCMS one year to handle the responsibility. Dale's prophecy of "a heavy agenda ahead" was certainly on the mark. By his 1964 installation as executive secretary of the International Convention he was serving simultaneously as president of the UCMS, executive secretary of the International Convention, and as administrative secretary of the commission on restructure. Holding these three offices placed him in the compelling position of diplomatically prodding the commission processes to develop the proposal, judiciously guiding the convention processes to approve the proposal, and wisely shaping a smooth transition from the UCMS in order to implement the proposal. Many throughout the Disciples then and now agree that Dale's balanced and thoughtful statesmanship in these positions was absolutely essential to the success of restructure. He was particularly skilled at adjudicating personal clashes within the leadership and at influencing the spirit of the process. This was his single most important personal ministry to the church, his finest hour. His greatest achievement, believed Kenneth Teegarden, was helping the church conceive and live into its new design.

In August 1964, Dale reported in a news release to the brotherhood that the council of agencies had concurred with the recommendation of the commission on brotherhood restructure to ask the International Convention board of directors to become an assembly of voting representatives, thereby changing the mass gathering to a delegate body. A month earlier the third full meeting of the commission had been held in Louisville. Ronald Osborn had delivered three lectures that were as important in shaping the nature of the church developed through restructure as Willard Wickizer's address was in launching the process. Osborn's lectures helped the commission develop the general principles that would characterize the newly restructured church. The structure would be designed so that the Christian Church (Disciples of Christ) in all its manifestations would reflect oneness; it would follow the principles of representative government through the structuring of delegate bodies; the national manifestation would have representation from local congregations and from regions; and it would express its unity through a covenantal relationship. At that same meeting the commission appointed a subcommittee (Ronald Osborn, William Barnett Blakemore, W.A. Welsh, Granville Walker, Albert Pennybacker, and George Beazley) to develop a provisional design.[30] The content of the provisional design was largely the work of these six men, although others contributed.

It was, in many ways, exactly the kind of church Dale had long dreamed. "The kind of Church we envisioned," Dale stated in an interview years later, "was one consistent with the nature of the Church as revealed in the New Testament and one that was true to the best in our Disciple's heritage especially our historic emphasis upon the unity and the wholeness of the Church in God's design: It was a church which manifests itself within the church universal; it was a church identifiable by name and manifesting its life and mission in congregations, regions, and the United States and Canada. It would be bound together as one in a covenantal relationship; it would be an ecumenical body. The name itself would indicate this. The identifiable aspects of this Church would be parenthetical as a sign that this church looked forward to the time when it 'would sink into union with the whole body of Christ on earth'".[31]

Shortly after Dale was installed as executive secretary of the International Convention, Kenneth L. Teegarden was appointed to succeed Dale as administrative secretary to the commission on brotherhood restructure. He was a native Oklahoman, a graduate of Phillips University—both B.A. and M.A.—and a B.D. graduate of Brite Divinity School. He had served pastorates in Oklahoma, Arkansas, and Texas but at the time was executive secretary of the Arkansas Christian Missionary Society and a member of the commission on brotherhood restructure. Kenneth was a significant contributor to the subcommittee charged with developing a provisional design. He was thin of stature, and in later years while general minister and president, he often presented himself as, "Exhibit A in your desire to have a lean general office." He began his work by reading everything Alexander Campbell had written on church organization, which was a formidable task and which he claimed was a very important influence on his thought. One of his favorite Campbell writings was the mythical story of founding a church on the Island of Guernsey and how it evolved organizationally, essentially Presbyterian in design, so congregations could counsel together. One Saturday in 1982, Kenneth was visiting with friends in St. Louis and recalled the story. He spent two hours discussing how it had influenced his thought during the restructure discussions and the meaning it held for our church in the 1980s. The incident illustrated the seriousness and thoroughness with which he approached the responsibility of his restructure assignment, still mulling over the meaning of that story twenty years later.[32]

Meetings to consider restructure were held in every state in 1965, along with thirteen regional assemblies. It was estimated that fifteen thousand Disciples participated in those events. Kenneth Teegarden attended most of them, answering questions in great detail. The general principles emerging from the 1964 Louisville meeting were ultimately placed before the 1966 International Convention in Dallas where, following spirited debate, they were passed. A provisional general assembly was approved for the following year in St. Louis where the design would be presented. The 1967 convention, after highly animated debate, did in fact give approval to the directions for the provisional design. Between that convention and the one scheduled for Kansas City in 1968, the states and agencies were to approve the document. Two-thirds had to act favorably if restructure was to proceed. They registered a strong favorable vote, and the Kansas City gathering vote was almost unanimous. The Christian Churches (Disciples of Christ) had been reconstituted into the Christian Church (Disciples of Christ). Dropping the *es* from Churches was a major philosophical and theological step.[33]

But it did not happen without serious opposition. Differences of opinion were expected, and they were carefully considered all the way through the process with the will of the majority being accepted. One group, Disciples for mission and renewal, was led by Charles Bayer whose opposition was based on their belief that the commission was addressing the wrong problem: "I really didn't think our problem was ecclesiology. I thought our problem was the loss of our sense of mission. It was the mission of the church that I hoped would be captured in restructure and not simply an organizational design that would parallel us with other churches . . . I made a rather severe attack on the whole process in the name of what I believed to be much more fundamental . . . I referred to our problem as a heart problem, not as an orthopedic problem. Simply getting the bones right wasn't going to help us." Charles' position was debated vigorously. This group did not really oppose restructure. They wanted it to go much further, a radical restructure. In the final analysis, Charles thought he and his group were not very effective, but "at least we had a platform."[34]

Another group, calling itself the committee for the preservation of the brotherhood, was located in Canton, Ohio, and was led by James DeForest Murch. It represented the independent point of view that had been critical of Disciples cooperative organizations for half a century. Murch, very active with the National Association of Evangelicals, was a reactionary Disciples minister who had been a persistent critic of all ecumenical initiatives including the Federal Council of Churches and both the national and world councils. This group wrote and distributed open letters to all the congregations. One was entitled, "Freedom or Restructure?" and the other, "The Truth about Restructure." The letters claimed that the new structure would take away the property rights of local congregations. The content was patently false and had almost no effect on cooperative congregations, but the marginal and uninformed congregations were confused. Congregational property rights were never in jeopardy but the willfully misleading claims, published and widely circulated, planted suspicions that would ultimately cause many congregations to withdraw.

A third group was the Atlanta declaration committee led by Robert Burns and Robert W. Shaw. Burns was a member of the commission on brotherhood restructure and past president of the international convention. He became deeply concerned about congregational rights and when the commission could not immediately act on his concerns he formed the Atlanta declaration committee. It contained leaders with strong cooperative commitments but whose platform was steeped in traditional anti-ecclesiasticism and the limitation of restructure to the agencies alone, preserving congregational freedom. The committee published and distributed a document containing its convictions and concerns which included inflammatory accusations, including the charge that the administrative committee would become an ecclesiastical court—there would be bishops, congregations would be controlled and their property rights endangered, a professional order of the ministry with hierarchical overtones would emerge, as would an unscriptural use of "Church."[35] Looking back on restructure, Burns reflected, "Restructure was fine that they put together. I made the motion to approve the provisional design. I could go along with it. I stayed in the Disciples. I'm still in the Year Book. I'm part of this gang. Born and bred in this briar patch." But then he added, "Restructure set us in a rigid pattern of functioning." And he also believed that the Atlanta opposition effort forced the guarantee of autonomy for local congregations, even though there is not a sign of evidence in the literature and reports that it was ever in question.[36]

Dale received hundreds of letters during those years criticizing his position on restructure. He answered the overwhelming majority of them. The following excerpt from a letter received just seven months prior to the vote at the September 1968 Kansas City assembly is typical:

> Your attack upon individualism and autonomous congregationalism reveals that you are fighting against the nineteenth-

century belief that a multiplicity of structureless individuals united under some kind of romantic idealism . . . cannot carry the burden of this hard time [and] has to be replaced by a pattern of responsible relationships at every level of the Christian Church. It is this displacement of faith in "individuals" for a faith in "structure" [that I protest.] . . . Too much world outreach talk is still nineteenth-century romantic idealism when the world was still available to the missionary. Of all persons, Dale, you know this is gone . . . Restructure abandons us to the desert shores of a vacant past. More seriously it abandons our basic insights into the experience of our western culture. Most seriously, it denies the spirit of a creative advance for the Christian mission . . . The church must be free, not restructured. It will be the poor, the stranger, the helpless, the lame, the blind, the victims of structure and the structureless of this world who will inherit the earth. Those, like Herod and Pilate, already committed to the finite forms of this world as universal will become the tyrants of the new age. Even John the Baptist will go into the kingdom last. And so shall we, Dale, and so shall we.[37]

In spite of this almost daily flow of criticism he sustained his strength of spirit.

Despite all the opposition, all the negative criticism, the restructure process achieved its major objectives. Disciples would no longer have to deny denominational existence. They had become a Church, with representative and delegated bodies. But the change was not so dramatic in structure as it was in the use of ecclesiological language to define the structures. Most of the membership and leadership of the commission on brotherhood restructure and its central committee were clergy, experienced in state and national cooperative organizations, devoted ecumenists who were active in both the World and National Councils of Churches, members or ministers of large urban congregations, educated in non-Disciples seminaries—sociological characteristics typical of cooperative Disciples leaders since 1900. These sociological characteristics profoundly conditioned their thought, freed them from instinctive respect for traditional patterns of Disciples organization, and encouraged them to re-create the accepted forms of church government, polity, and authority into a new expression of Church. It was, however, the extra-local cooperative life of Disciples that they represented and that they restructured. Organizational continuity and leadership continuity were more pronounced results of restructure than organizational change or leadership change. The restructure process did not create new structures so much as it claimed churchly status for those already in existence beyond the congregation. In the final analysis, Dale's great dream of "Church" was achieved. The principle act of restructure was the Christian Church (Disciples of Christ). The very name, Christian Church (Disciples of Christ), provides the most grand and eloquent summary of the restructure process.[38] A single generation of leaders had transformed the church and reorganized familiar components into a new structure. Future generations will inherit and build on their achievement.

The September 28, 1968, vote was the most significant action organizationally for Disciples in 136 years. Moderator Ronald Osborn called for the vote after twelve amendments had been considered, five approved and seven defeated. The final vote was overwhelmingly approved and followed by thirty seconds of applause. Then Osborn asked Bill Guthrie to lead the singing of the Doxology. The theme of that assembly was "We Rejoice in God," a phrase lifted from the provisional design, and the people in that moment truly rejoiced.[39]

Dale's view of the result deserves to be heard. Responding in written form to a series of questions from T.J. Liggett in 1999, Dale expressed his opinion on the outcome of restructure. To the question "What was achieved?" Dale responded:

> The Dream of becoming Church and transcending the society concept was gloriously achieved. I think the way it was done and what was done constituted a fresh and creative approach to church structure and mission. When we went to the law firm for incorporation, the firm said to us—"the corporation laws of any one state would be shabby raiment for so grand a conception of the Church." Another unique achievement was the basis of membership in the church. The region does not consist of member congregations nor the general manifestation of member regions. Each person is a member of all three. All are linked together by covenant and by representative government.[40]

To the question, "Where did we fall short?" Dale responded:

> It was in the process of dismantling our existing programmatic and promotional structures and integrating their functions into the new church structure. There were a number of minefields, and we stepped on a few in doing it. We fell short on integrating the regional manifestations of the church, but I don't know that we could have done differently at the time. The three manifestations evolved as I expected but not with the esprit de corps I had hoped.

To the question, "What price did we pay?" Dale responded:

> We lost a lot of momentum in the areas of program planning and promotion. I think a tremendous price was paid in the breakup of the United Society. I am sure it was the right thing to do, but my heart aches every time I think of it. It was

absolutely essential to the full realization of the 'Dream.' Virgil Sly and T.J. Liggett are to be credited with the most magnificent demonstration of the surrender of position, power, and prestige I have ever witnessed. We lost twenty-seven hundred congregations. Sadly, this was part of the price. [It should be noted that the loss of congregations was a loss in membership and unity, not a loss of financial support. Total giving actually increased the year following restructure because the congregations that left had long been critical of the brotherhood and had not supported it financially for several decades.]

To the question, "What have we learned?" Dale responded:

T'ain't easy! The restructure process was right and necessary. We were on target in building into the design provision for continuing reform and renewal. And we learned it is a recurring need to interpret the "dream" to each new generation lest we forget its primary objective to be a worthy manifestation of Church within the Church Universal.

To the question, "What is the major unfinished task?" Dale responded:

The development of church-wide strategies for mission and planning programs to accomplish it. This is likely a responsibility of the general board. The other is the promotion and financing of the church's mission. We have struggled with this for thirty years. Time after time proposals have been shot down, usually by regional resistance and at times educational institutions.

In his state of the church address to the 1968 Kansas City assembly Dale offered a benedictory conclusion to the long and arduous process. He told those assembled the church could not deal with structure, mission, and renewal in isolation from each other. He expressed his conviction that the brotherhood had been led by the spirit to develop a more theologically and pragmatically sound structure. Then he ended the long quest with the words, "I pray that we will bring to the mission new resources of commitment and spiritual power which arise out of an obedient response to the divine call to be the church."[41]

General Minister and President: 1968–1973

By the rules and procedures established in the provisional design, Dale was elected from a pool of candidates at the 1968 Kansas City General Assembly to one job with a long title—General Minister and President of the Christian Church (Disciples of Christ) in the United States and Canada—the longest title in Protestantism. Facing him was the major task of implementing the newly restructured church and providing effective leadership to a new denomination in what soon was identified as a post-denominational world. The first order of business was dismantling the UCMS. It generated sharp opposition among several staff members and created concern in the minds of other church members. Helen Spaulding remembered it as a dreadful moment. "Virgil Sly [was] a very generous statesman. He said the United Society would divide its assets. We do not want to be one huge overbalancing unit of the new church. We will divide. We will give our headquarters building to the general organization without charge. I thought Virgil was giving away the whole thing, and I was very concerned about it. But I respected his feeling that he wanted us to do something to lead in helping achieve the goals of restructure."[42] Dividing the UCMS into the Division of Overseas Ministries, the Division of Homeland Ministries, and a Christian Church Services unit (i.e., communications, Year Book, building maintenance, etc.) along with the transfer of capital, personnel, and other responsibilities to the general church and to the new regions was a monumental and controversial act.

In October 1968 Virgil Sly retired as president, and T. J. Liggett became the last president of the UCMS and the one who presided over the asset division, finally completed in 1971. Dale participated in T.J.'s inauguration and provided oversight for the structural changes. Upon his retirement, Virgil wrote to Dale, "I don't know when two men have had the opportunity of being colleagues on the executive level, who have maintained such a wonderful friendship and understanding as we have during these years."[43] In a way Virgil's letter added a final handshake to a chapter of Dale's ministry, a time he would always cherish.

Implementation was indeed a time-consuming matter. Preparation for new plenary sessions at the next assembly had to be planned. Bringing the general board and administrative committee into existence had to be quickly accomplished. The withdrawal of nearly twenty-seven hundred congregations had to be managed gingerly. Building a sense of church

Dale as general minister and president, 1968; left to right, Gertrude Dimke, Kenneth Teegarden, Dale Fiers, James Suggs, Howard Dentler, and Bob Friedly.

wholeness within the cabinet was also a significant challenge. Kenneth Teegarden and Gertrude Dimke both remembered the early cabinet meetings convened by Dale, without any real guidance from the design, as quite difficult. Some of the agency heads had not been enthusiastically supportive of restructure. According to Kenneth, "They said essentially we want to cooperate, but we have our own task to perform—Dale was very patient with them."[44] This same feeling was equally pronounced when he attempted to bring cohesion to the body of regional ministers, again without any real guidance from the design. It was also Dale's responsibility to give definition to his title, general minister and president. Teegarden recalled, "Dale shaped the title; his style of ministry was reflected in it; he was both pastoral and administrative in his nature; and he applied this title to his staff as a whole. There was no sense of personal promotion; you could never question his honesty; there was never a question about who he was. He was a strong and obvious leader, but not a domineering or dominating administrator. He was thought of primarily as a minister with caring concern for others and a deep commitment to 'church.'"[45]

Dale invested considerable effort in an attempt to mount a capital campaign for mission within the newly constituted church. The needs were assembled from all units of the church and a goal of $200,000,000 established. Before the campaign could be launched it had to be approved and internal conflicts among regions, general units, and educational institutions caused the church to draw back from the effort. "This failure," said Dale, "was one of my bitter disappointments. My sad conclusion was that we were not yet enough of a church to make a church-wide effort."[46] A second early failure was the attempt to develop an all-church curriculum on Discipleship. Obviously, time would be required to evolve into the "oneness" Dale envisioned.

One of the intentions of restructure was to replace autonomy with covenant. Some believe congregations, general units, and regions emerged from the restructure process with less than a full understanding of the new covenantal relationship. Dale activated the cabinet and the council of ministers to interpret restructure as well as to coordinate ministry. But neither the general units nor the regions developed an effective, sustained teaching role to help imbue Disciples with a more thorough understanding of covenant or the meaning of Church. Consequently, congregations, regions, and general units all remained a bit unsure of the new structure, causing an initial tentativeness in the early attempts to become Church. This was symbolized by the failures of the curriculum and capital campaign efforts. Moving from autonomy to covenant and toward becoming Church was a complicated, frustrating, and long-term process. Time would be required to overcome hard, deep-rooted traditions.

In addition to an almost overwhelming number of administrative chores, Dale was responsible for representing the new church to a national and international public. He is to be credited with conceiving the idea of "Reconciliation," the urban emergency program. The response of the new church was both heartening and prophetic. The Reconciliation Fund, launched in 1968, still exists and is used to combat racism. In that year Dale was quoted in the *Los Angeles Times* as saying, "Churchmen showed more concern with secular movements that work for justice and peace than with talk of unity. The latter sounds empty in the face of pressing world problems." He conceded, "This attitude presents a paradox at a time when there is a new understanding of the oneness of the church."[47]

The war in Vietnam was as divisive within the church as in all other areas of American society. When the United States bombed Cambodia in May 1970, Dale wrote to President Richard Nixon, supporting the president's action as not being a de facto escalation and he accepted the sincerity and stated objectives that he understood to be hastening an end to the war and strengthening chances for a negotiated peace. He also told the president that others within the church thought the war had been

escalated and that the president was not sensing the mood of many citizens on this issue. On June 3, 1970, Dale was handed a petition signed
by fifty-four members of the national staff sharply disagreeing with
Dale's position. He replied that he "respected the right to speak by his
staff members and recognized their position as one of conscience . . . I'm
glad they felt free to send the petition to me."[48] Just three weeks later, on
June 26, he was handed another petition signed by seventy national staff
and office employees supporting his stand and saying, "Thank God you
have the courage of your convictions."[49]

Taking a stand on controversial issues became common fare. The
importance of social justice issues and the need to take a moral stand were
instilled in him long ago at Yale. At the 1971 Assembly in Louisville
Dale told those assembled, "We are going to make some decisions on
substantive and even divisive issues."[50] He said that it was necessary for
the church to take a stand on issues of social justice within a moral and
theological context. Two years later he headed a list of Disciples leaders
who signed a statement supporting the Equal Rights Amendment.
He again wrote President Nixon regarding another phase of renewed
bombing, "expressing disillusionment and urging other means to end
the war."[51] He questioned the practical effect of the bombing as well as
its morality and urged a military withdrawal. Eighty members of the
general staff endorsed Dale's message. Some person or some group
inevitably criticized each public stand Dale took, but the Christian
Church (Disciples of Christ) was beginning to realize that at times it was
speaking as a church through Dale. He understood the gravity of this
responsibility and accepted the criticism.

The 1973 General Assembly held in Cincinnati would be the last for
Dale as general minister and president. The moment was marked by the
election of Walter Bingham as moderator, the first African American to
hold the position. It was an event of paramount significance for Dale,

given his long and extensive work with civil rights. The assembly invested considerable time debating health care and migrant worker proposals. But the indelible memory for all who were there was telling Dale and Betty good-bye. More than three thousand persons attended the retirement dinner honoring the Fierses. A drama troupe paid special tribute to them with a "This is your Life" sketch and the singing of "Auld Lang Syne."

And then suddenly it was time for retirement. It hardly seemed possible. Although there had been detractors, it was difficult for most to imagine the church without Dale and Betty Fiers at the helm. They had pioneered the role of general minister and president and led the transition to a more churchly church. By all conventional standards of measurement, A. Dale Fiers was the most important Disciples leader of the twentieth century. He and Betty were honored in many different settings but perhaps the most meaningful was "Dale Fiers Day" in Hamilton, Ohio. The mayor, Frank Witt, proclaimed the day in honor of Dale's retirement. High Street Christian Church had been his first pastorate following graduation from seminary in 1935, nearly forty years before. It was at High Street Christian Church, on October 28, 1973, that he preached his last sermon as general minister and president. Three hundred persons attended the service, including twelve whom Dale baptized during his ministry at Hamilton. Dale had come full circle in his ministry and what a magnificent journey it had been. No one among Disciples enjoyed more respect. How fitting to conclude his truly extraordinary ministry of forty years in the county seat congregation where it all began.[52]

❖ ❖ ❖ ❖ ❖ ❖ ❖ ❖ ❖ ❖ ❖ ❖ ❖ ❖ ❖

Epilogue

The Fiers retired in "the house that Dale built" on Singer Island, Palm Beach Shores, Florida. It was fondly called "Scene by the Sea." Here they frequently sailed on their boat, *The Betty K,* and fished the deep sea. Scene by the Sea was the favorite family gathering place for holidays and special occasions, generally highlighted by Hugh Joyce and Dale regaling the relatives with piano and banjo duets. Their Palm Beach home also served as the planning headquarters for the seniors retreat program that Dale and Betty organized and led for the region of Florida. Betty led the singing and Dale played his banjo. Most often, Dale and Betty spent the summer months at their cabin near Crystal Lake, Michigan.

A man of his energy and talent, however, could not remain totally idle. Almost immediately he was invited to chair the National City Christian Church Foundation Board, which he accepted. He would hold this position for more than a decade during the restoration years for National City Christian Church. Simultaneously he began serving congregational interims, beginning at First Christian Church in Naples and then a second one at North Dade Christian Church in Miami. The third of his postretirement pastorates was First Christian Church (1976–1977) in Miami, Florida. It was a historic congregation, once served by Everett Smith. This congregation had parented North Dade Christian Church, University Christian Church, Coral Gables Christian Church, and Broadway Christian Church. Robert Shaw was also part of the Miami First history and had been critical of Dale during restructure, describing him as the personification of all that was wrong with the church. There is a certain grace attached to the fact that Dale reached an age to return and to be remembered in such a beloved way for helping the congregation create a permanent legacy for its rich heritage.[1]

He served a fourth interim at Parkway Christian Church in Plantation, Florida, where he was remembered for his "wonderful sermons" and his highly professional and ethical behavior regarding the search for a permanent minister. One Parkway parishioner recalled that when Dale came to you and placed his hand firmly on your shoulder and asked you to do something for the church—"How could you say no?—it was like being in God's presence with his hand resting on your shoulder."

Park Avenue Christian Church (1977–1978) in New York City then issued a call. Dale telephoned Betty from a Chicago general board meeting, where he was attending as former general minister and president and where he had just received an invitation to the interim assignment. He told Betty he thought God was calling him to Park Avenue. Betty responded, "Well, I haven't heard God calling me!" The congregation was struggling, and some advised Dale not to go, actually recommending the church be closed. But Dale and Betty accepted the call along with the challenges accompanying it.

Hampton Adams had come to Dale when he was still president of the UCMS asking help to build an educational building at Park Avenue. Dale convinced the Christian Board of Publication and the UCMS to guarantee a bond issue for $1,000,000 to build the building. When Dale became interim minister at Park Avenue, the congregation still owed $400,000 on that debt. Shortly after his arrival, Dale called on Clementine Tangeman. She agreed to provide a two-for-one challenge to launch a campaign to pay off the $400,000 debt. Not only was the debt liquidated but also a trustees fund was established. Dale and Betty made the initial gift to the fund.

At Park Avenue, Dale learned to be a pastor by telephone. People, he said, did not really want you to visit in their home, but a telephone call was fine. So they telephoned every member of the congregation, much to the surprise of many. Dale remembered Park Avenue as an exceptionally rewarding interim ministry.[2]

In 1981 Dale and Betty celebrated their fiftieth wedding anniversary. Alan and Barbara provided a reception for them in Florida. They were

Dale and Betty on their fiftieth wedding anniversary, 1981

also honored at special occasions in Cleveland, Crystal Beach, Indianapolis, New York, and Washington DC. It was a golden wedding year filled with celebration.

Dale served his sixth interim at Seventh Street Christian Church (1985) in Richmond, Virginia. Barbara and Hugh Joyce were active members of the congregation. It was the first time Dale served a congregation where his family was among the membership, since his children were young. Seventh Street had not had a balanced budget in six years. Dale activated the stewardship department and conducted an every-member canvas. They went over the budget goal when the last pledge came in at $6,000. Everyone rejoiced. Dale remembered it as a very satisfying interim.[3]

The Fiers' faith was tested in the fall of 1992. Their daughter, Barbara, died of cancer. She had been fighting it for several years. Bearing the loss in a way that strengthened their faith was a Fiers trademark. Dale was asked to speak at her graveside. "It was Barbara's express wish to be buried here, near the Old Mill that has stood by the flowing waters of the Little River for 172 years. From the Old Mill, which was transformed into her much loved art studio, came a steady stream of beauty in pen and ink and watercolor expressing the beauty of her mind and heart . . . It is entirely fitting that the offices of faith and love should be performed here . . . surrounded by the family and friends she held so dear."[4]

In February of 1997 Betty was diagnosed with pancreatic cancer. The valiant struggle she waged was an inspiration to everyone. It was said that Betty and Dale were for each other, and all who knew them, a truly magnificent witness to Christian faith and to faithfulness in marriage. In her final months she wrote a brief story of her life as a gift for Dale, which she closed by saying, "For sixty-seven years you have been the love and joy of my life! I remember our sixty-seven years of life together. Thanks be to God for those years—for our family, our friends and a good life."[5]

She died peacefully in her sleep on June 26, 1998, just sixteen days before their sixty-seventh wedding anniversary.

Dale was ninety-two years old at the time of Betty's death, yet his life was still vigorous. Among other responsibilities he was an active member of Riverside Avenue Christian Church in Jacksonville, Florida. The congregation was searching for a minister, and invited Dale to serve as a consultant to the search committee. The chair of the committee was the recently widowed Virginia Sponaugle. Dale was impressed with her skill in managing the search. Following Betty's death, Dale and Virginia found themselves serving on several Riverside committees together. A common involvement with and a mutual love for the church drew them together. On June 17, 2000, they married. At age ninety-four Dale drove Virginia from Florida to Michigan and back for their honeymoon trip. Both Virginia and Dale said how fortunate they felt "to have found each other, to care for each other." In December 2002, Virginia was diagnosed with a malignant brain tumor. Following several weeks of what Dale described as a courageous struggle, she died early on the morning of February 3, 2003.

On October 28, 2000 Dale delivered, by his own definition, a "farewell address" at the regional assembly in West Palm Beach, Florida, near his boyhood home. The address was a reflection on his sixty years of ministry. "Just seventy-five years ago," he began, "my mother and father, two sisters, and some church friends took me to the railroad station here in West Palm Beach. I boarded the train for a two-and-one-half-day trip over four railroad systems and the Toonerville Trolley to enroll in Bethany College and prepare for ministry . . . If anyone had told me where ministry would take me I would have laughed and said, 'You are out of your mind!'" [Four Ohio pastorates; thirteen years as president of the UCMS; executive secretary of the commission on brotherhood restructure; executive secretary of the international convention; the first general minister and president; and six interim pastorates in postretirement]. He then spoke of the lessons he had learned during his sixty years of ministry. The one with the greatest impact on him,

> . . . . was the local congregation [as] the indispensable foundation of the church's witness and mission in the world. My sixty plus years in the ministry were almost equally divided between being a pastor of congregations and being involved in the general ministries of our church. It was in the latter capacity that I came to comprehend fully the strategic importance of the congregation in the accomplishment of the church's mission on earth. Time and time again as I traveled over the nation and around the world I marveled at what was happening because of local congregations like those I had been privileged to serve. They were the source of ministers that filled the pulpits, missionaries that go to the far corners of the earth, dedicated lay people that staff our boards and institutions, individuals who provide the money to support the worldwide enterprise of Christ. The success of the restructured Christian Church will depend upon the extent to which local Disciples congregations become headquarters for mission that reaches from the doorstep to the ends of the earth.[6]

At this writing, A. Dale Fiers has reached the ninety-sixth anniversary of his birth. His remarkably long and extraordinarily profound ministry continues through the thoughtful counsel he so graciously shares with those who come into his presence seeking to know the gift of his spirit. On the fortieth anniversary of his ordination and near the time of his retirement Dale preached a sermon in which he affirmed the reward of a lifetime in ministry:

Dale Fiers and D. Duane Cummins in front of Alexander Campbell's gravestone

I am grateful for my call to the ministry of the Christian Church (Disciples of Christ). I rejoice in the heritage which I received in preparation for a lifetime of ministry....For me the concern for the unity of the church has been an expanding and developing one across the years. My understanding of its complexities, and involvement in its expressions of cooperation, and the quest for union has been fulfilling, exciting and rewarding beyond measure![7]

Fiers Geneaological Chart

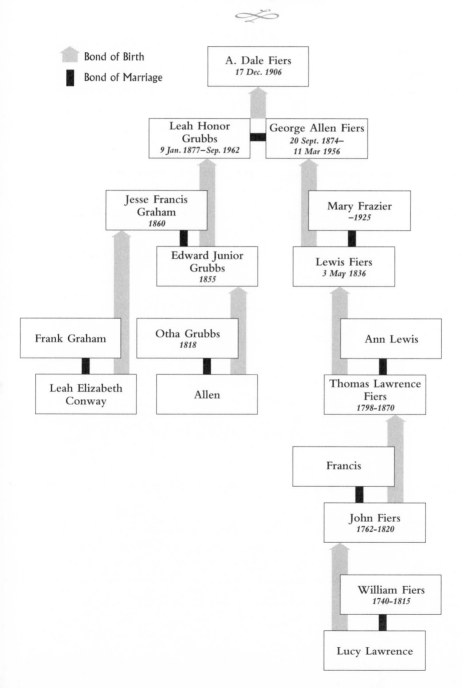

Bond of Birth

Bond of Marriage

A. Dale Fiers
17 Dec. 1906

Leah Honor
Grubbs
9 Jan. 1877–Sep. 1962

George Allen Fiers
*20 Sept. 1874–
11 Mar 1956*

Jesse Francis
Graham
1860

Mary Frazier
–1925

Edward Junior
Grubbs
1855

Lewis Fiers
3 May 1836

Frank Graham

Otha Grubbs
1818

Ann Lewis

Leah Elizabeth
Conway

Allen

Thomas Lawrence
Fiers
1798-1870

Francis

John Fiers
1762-1820

William Fiers
1740-1815

Lucy Lawrence

Chute/Kunz Geneaological Chart

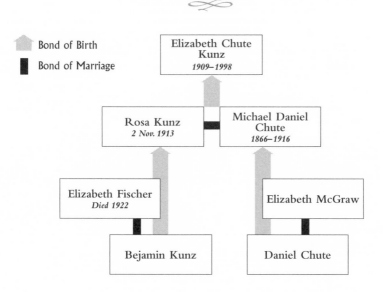

Bond of Birth

Bond of Marriage

Elizabeth Chute
Kunz
1909–1998

Rosa Kunz
2 Nov. 1913

Michael Daniel
Chute
1866–1916

Elizabeth Fischer
Died 1922

Elizabeth McGraw

Bejamin Kunz

Daniel Chute

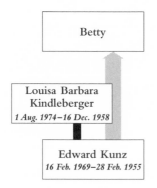

Betty

Louisa Barbara
Kindleberger
1 Aug. 1974–16 Dec. 1958

Edward Kunz
16 Feb. 1969–28 Feb. 1955

Fiers Chronology

1896	Marriage of George Fiers and Leah Grubbs
1906	Birth of A. Dale Fiers
1909	Birth of Elizabeth Chute Kunz
1929	Graduated from Bethany; Ordained into ministry;
	Selected pastor of Shadyside Christian Church, Ohio
1931	Marriage of Dale Fiers and Betty Kunz
	Enrolled at Yale Divinity School
1935	Graduated from Yale Divinity School
	Pastor High Street Christian Church, Hamilton, Ohio
1936	Birth of Barbara Fiers, daughter of Dale and Betty
1939	Pastor Central Christian Church, Newark, Ohio
	Birth of Allen Fiers, son of Dale and Betty
1946	Elected to board of directors of United Christian Missionary Society
	Elected to board of trustees of Bethany College
	Elected program chairman for the International Convention
	Elected chairman of the board of UCMS
	President of the Cleveland Church Federation
1951	Elected president of the UCMS
1952	World tour of mission fields
1953	Publication of *This is Missions*
1954	Elected to the general board of the National Council of Churches

1960   Betty appointed to Indiana State Civil Rights Commission by governor

Publication of *Lord, Teach us to Pray*

1961   Publication of *Prayer in the Great Decisions of Life*

Attended Third Assembly of World Council of Churches

1966   Dallas convention—general principles for restructure approved

Publication of *The Christian World Mission*

1968   Elected first general minister and president of the newly restructured church

1973   Retirement to Scene by the Sea at West Palm Beach

Interim Minister at First Christian Church, Naples

2001   Dale Fiers honored by Disciples of Christ Historical Society at the Kansas City General Assembly

Chapter One: The Fiers 1740–1906

1. Camus, Albert, "The Wrong Side and the Right Side," *Lyrical and Critical Essays*. (New York: Vintage Books, 1968), p. 60.

2. Howard, Robert P., *Illinois: A History of the Prairie State*. (Grand Rapids, Michigan: Eerdman's Publishing, 1972), pp. 224, 260;   Kankakee County History: *http://www.prairienet.org/fordiroq/kankakee/history.htm;* Kankakee History: *http://www.rootsweb.com/~ilkankak/history/k3histo6/k30616a;* Kankakee Map: *http://tigr.census.gov/cgo-bin/mapsurger?lat=41.11000 & lon=87.9000*.

3. Clark, Kenneth, "Provincialism," *Moments of Vision*. (London: J. Murray, 1981), pp. 50-62. Bailyn, Bernard. *To Begin the World Anew*. (New York: Knopf, 2003) pp. 6-7.

4. Fiers, Russel D., "Fiers Family Newsletter." Issue #3, Oct. 31, 1992, p. 4.

   Fiers, Russel D. to A. Dale Fiers. July 11, 1991.

   Genforum: *http://genforum.genealogy.com/fiers/* posted by George Simmons, Oct. 16, 1998.

5. Fiers Newsletter, pp. 4-6.

6. Ibid. pp. 6-8; Genforum; Madison, James H. *The Indiana Way: A State History*. (Indianapolis: Indiana University Press, 1986), pp. 95-98; Milton, Jay. *History of Jay County, Indiana,* Vol. II, (Indianapolis: Historical Publishing Company, 1922), pp. 362-363.

7. Fiers Newsletter, p. 8; Pierson, Darrol, to Bethany Library, May 19, 2000, pp. 2-3. (Indiana State Library); Bureau of the Census, 1880 Illinois Census. F620. District 126, Sheet 18, Line 2; Report of the Adjutant General of Indiana. 19th IVI. Vol. 4 (1861-1865), p. 406-07; 19th Regiment Indiana Volunteers: *http://19th Indiana.com/19thhist.html;* K Company, 19th Regiment, *http://home.att.net/~b.c.henry/page4.html;* Nolan, Alan T., *The Iron Brigade*. (Indianapolis: Indiana University Press, 1994), passim; Civil War Muster Rolls: State Archives of Indiana. Madison, p. 197-198; McCormick, David. *A Record of Indiana Organizations in the Mexican, Civil and Spanish-American Wars*. (Indianapolis: n.p., 1929), pp. 5-6; 151-156.

8. Fiers, Alan, to D. Duane Cummins, August 22, 2000.

9. 1880 Illinois Census. District 126, Sheet 18, Line 2; Interview with A. Dale Fiers by D. Duane Cummins, August 16, 1999.

10. Edward Junior Grubbs and Jesse Grubbs to Othel Brown, 1940; Fiers, interview, August 16, 1999.

11. Fiers, interview, August 16, 1999.

12. Ibid.

13. Memorial tribute to Leah Honor (Grubbs) Fiers, 1962, p. 1.

14. Illinois marriages Index. *http://www2.sos.state.il.us/cgi-bin/marriage* p. 00007602; Leah Fiers tribute, p. 2.

15. Leah Fiers tribute. p. 4.

16. Ibid. p. 3-5.

17. Brands, H. W., T. R. *The Last Romantic*. (New York: Basic Books, 1997), pp. 586-593; Mowry, George E., *The Era of Theodore Roosevelt*. (New York: Harper & Row, 1958), passim.

18. Morison, Samuel Eliot, Henry Steele Commager, and William Leuchtenburg. *The Growth of the American Republic,* Vol. II, (New York: Oxford University Press, 1980), pp. 266-294.

19. Wilson, A. N., *God's Funeral*. (New York: Norton & Co., 1999), pp. 3-21.

20. Pelikan, Jaroslav, *Jesus Through the Centuries*. (New Haven: Yale University Press, 1985), pp. 182-206.

21. Garrison, W. E., and Alfred DeGroot. *The Disciples of Christ: A History*. (St. Louis: Bethany Press, 1948, 1958), pp. 383-412; Harrell, David. *The Social Sources of Division in the Disciples of Christ 1865-1900*. (Atlanta: Publishing Systems, 1973), pp. 1-32; Stump, Roger W. "Spatial Patterns of Growth & Decline Among Disciples 1890-1980," in Williams, Newell, *A Case Study of Mainstream Protestantism*. (St. Louis: Chalice Press, 1991), pp. 451-452; Tucker, William E., and Lester McAllister, *Journey in Faith*. (St. Louis: Bethany Press, 1975), pp. 284-307.

Chapter Two: Childhood to Marriage 1906–1931

1. Furia, Judith, *100 Years in the History of Kankakee*. (Kankakee, Illinois: Kankakee County Historical Society, 1999), p. 1-2: Kankakee Photographs (1900, 1924?); Judith Furia to D. Duane Cummins, June 29, 2000.

2. A. Dale Fiers, interview by D. Duane Cummins, February 18, 2000; A. Dale Fiers, interview by D. Duane Cummins, July 2, 2000.

3. Kankakee City Directories, 1902, 1904, 1909, 1916.

4. *http://clubs.hemmings.com/clubsites/hupmobile/history.htm*; Fiers, interview, July 2, 2000.

5. Judith Furia, "Kankakee History," (unpublished pamphlet), p. 2; A. Dale Fiers, interview by D. Duane Cummins, August 16, 1999.

6. Fiers, interview, July 2, 2000.

7. Fiers, interview, August 16, 1999; Fiers, interview, February 18, 2000; Fiers, interview, July 2, 2000; A. Dale Fiers, "A Biographical Sketch of Alan Dale Fiers," Unpublished, p. 1-2.

8. Donald W. Curl, *Palm Beach County*, (Palm Beach: Windsor Publications, 1986), p. 8.

9. United States Census 1900, 1910, 1920.

10. Fiers, interview, August 16,1999.

11. *Year Book of the Christian Church*. 1914, 1917; Fiers, interview, February 18, 2000; "Biographical Sketch," p. 2-3.

12. Ronald E. Osborn, "The Structure of Cooperation," *Mid-Stream,* Vol. II, No. 2. December 1962, p. 29; Tucker, William E., and Lester G. McAllister, *Journey in Faith*. (St. Louis: Bethany Press, 1975), pp. 344-349.

13. D. Duane Cummins, *A Handbook for Today's Disciples*. (St. Louis: Chalice Press, 1991), p. 10.

14. Fiers, interview, August 16, 1999; Fiers, interview, February 18, 2000; Fiers, interview, July 2, 2000; "A Biographical Sketch," p. 5.

15. "A Biographical Sketch," p. 3.

16. Ibid. p. 4.

17. A. Dale Fiers, "I Remember Palm Beach High School," Unpublished, (1 page), 1992.

18. Palm Beach High School transcript, 1925.

19. Articles clipped from the sports pages of the *Palm Beach Post* and placed in Dale's sports scrapbook by his mother.

20. Ibid.

21. Ibid.

22. Ibid.

23. Fiers, interview, July 2, 2000; Fiers, interview, August 16, 1999.

24. *Bethany College Catalogue*, 1925-26: Bethany College roster of students, 1928-29; W. K. Woolery, *Bethany Years*, (Cincinnati: Standard Publishing, 1941, pp 249-255); Lester G. McAllister, *Bethany: The First 150 Years*, (Bethany, West Virginia: Bethany College Press, 1991), p. 253-267.

25. William James, *Selected Papers on Philosophy*. (London: Everyman's Library, 1917), pp. 86-87.

26. Alfred North Whitehead, "The Aims of Education," *Alfred North Whitehead: An Anthology*. (New York: Macmillan, 1961), p. 97.

27. Bethany College transcript, A. Dale Fiers, 1929; *Bethany College Catalogue*, 1925-26, P. 35

28. William Leuchtenberg, *Perils of Prosperity*. (New York: Macmillan, 1958), pp. 149-157.

29. Fiers, interview, August 16, 1999; Fiers, interview, July 2, 2000.

30. Fiers, interview, August 16; Fiers, interview, July 2.

31. Forrest Kirkpatrick to Dale Fiers, November 28, 1925.

32. Leah Fiers to Forrest Kirkpatrick, March 27, 1926.

33. *The Bethanian*, 1926, 1927, 1928, 1929: Bethany sports scrapbook compiled by Dale's parents.

34. Bethany scrapbook.

35. McAllister, Lester, to D. Duane Cummins, June 14, 2002.

36. Class Day Program, Monday, 11 June 1929; Services of Ordination Program, Old Bethany Church, 11 June 1929.

37. Ordination Program.

38. Fiers, interview, August 16, 1999.

39. Minutes of the official board, Shadyside Christian Church, April 28, 1929.

40. *Year Book of the Christian Church*, 1929, 1931.

41. Minutes of the official board, Shadyside Christian Church, June 3, 1929-January 2, 1931; Fiers, interview, July 2, 2000.

42. Fiers, interview, July 2, 2000.

43. Elizabeth Kunz Fiers, "Memories of Childhood and Beyond," (unpublished), December 25, 1991, pp. 1-2.

44. Ibid, p. 5-6.

45. Ibid, p. 8.

46. Ibid, p. 19; Fiers, interview, August 16.

47. Fiers, interview, August 16.

Chapter Three: Yale to Euclid Avenue 1931–1951

1. A. Dale Fiers, interview by D. Duane Cummins, July 2, 2000.

2. A. Dale Fiers, interview by D. Duane Cummins, February 18, 2000.

3. *Bulletin of Yale University Divinity School,* 1931-1932, pp. 66-81; 81-84: A. Dale Fiers, interview by D. Duane Cummins, January 20, 2001.

4. Irvin T. Green to Luther Weigle, January 2, 1931.

5. Cloyd Goodnight to Luther Weigle, February 3, 1931.

6. Luther Weigle to A. Dale Fiers, September 23, 1931.

7. Roland Bainton, *Yale and the Ministry.* (New York: Harper & Row, 1957), p. 261.

8. Ibid, p. 262.

9. Conrad Cherry, *Hurrying Toward Zion: Universities, Divinity Schools & American Protestantism.* (Bloomington: Indiana University Press, 1995), pp. 29-30.

10. Roland Bainton, *Yale and the Ministry.* (New York: Harper & Row, 1957), p. 261.

11. Conrad Cherry, p. 152: see also, James W. Fraser, *Schooling the Preachers: The Redevelopment of Protestant Theological Education in the United States 1740-1875.* (New York: New York University Press, 1988) and Glenn T. Miller, *Piety & Intellect: The Aims & Purposes of Ante-Bellum Theological Education.* (Atlanta: Scholars Press, 1990).

12. Conrad Cherry, p. 141.

13. Ibid., p. 140: Roland Bainton, *Yale and the Ministry.* (New York: Harper & Row, 1957), p. 262.

14. *Bulletin of Yale University,* 1931, pp. 21; 20-40.

15. Fiers, interview, January 20, 2001.

16. Ibid.

17. A. Dale Fiers, "Credo," (unpublished), June 1, 1933, pp. 4-5.

18. Ibid, p. 6.

19. Ibid, pp. 11-12.

20. Ibid, p. 13.

21. Ibid, pp. 14-15.

22. Ibid, p. 16.

23. Ibid, p. 24.

24. Ibid.

25. Ibid, preface.

26. *Bulletin of Yale Divinity School, 1933*: A. Dale Fiers, Interview by D. Duane Cummins, 20 January 2001.

27. A. Dale Fiers, "The Unified Program and the Local Church," (unpublished,1934), p. 1; Fiers, interview, January 20, 2001.

28. *Bulletin of Yale Divinity School,* 1933; Fiers, interview by D. Duane Cummins, 20 January 2001.

29. A. Dale Fiers, "The Conflict between Christianity and Gnosticism," (Unpublished 1934), p. 4; A. Dale Fiers, "The Place of Pastoral Psychology in the Work of Ministry," (unpublished, 1934).

30. A. Dale Fiers, "Westermark's Theory of Ethical Relativity," (unpublished, 1934).

31. High Street Christian Church board minutes, 1935-1939, p. 12.

32. T. H. Watkins, *The Hungry Years.* (New York: Holt & Company, 1999), pp. 56-57.

33. Arthur Schlesinger, Jr., *The Crises of the Old Order.* (Boston: Houghton Mifflin, 1957), pp. 1-3

34. William, O. Paulsell, "The Disciples of Christ & the Great Depression," Unpublished Ph.D, Thesis, Vanderbilt 1965, pp. 143, 292, 441: William E. Tucker and Lester G. McAllister, *Journey in Faith,* (St. Louis: Bethany Press, 1975), pp. 288-400.

35. Tucker and McAllister, ibid.

36. Fiers, interview, July 2, 2000; Fiers, interview, January 20, 2001.

37. High Street minutes, 1935-1939, p. 15.

38. High Street minutes, pp. 12-15; Fiers, interview, August 16, 1999.

39. High Street minutes, pp. 12-15: Year Book, 1935, 1937.

40. *Year Book*, 1935, 1937.

41. Ibid. p. 16.

42. Fiers, interview, August 16, 1999.

43. *Newark Advocate & American Tribune*, 5 January 1939, p. 4.

44. *Year Book*, 1939, 1945; Fiers, interview, February 18, 2000.

45. *Newark Christian*, 15 June 1944, p. 1.

46. Fiers, interview, July 2, 2000.

47. A. Dale Fiers to "Fellows Overseas," June 8, 1942.

48. Fiers to Fellows, August 16, 1945.

49. Service of Thanksgiving Bulletin, Newark Central Church of Christ, August 15, 1945.

50. *Newark Advocate and American Tribune*, September 1945, p. 3.

51. Ibid; *News of the Brotherhood*, August 29, 1945.

52. *The Cleveland Plain Dealer*, October 4, 1945, p. 14.

53. Jacob H. Goldner to A. Dale Fiers, July 25, 1945

54. Gerould Goldner to A. Dale Fiers, August 21, 1945

55. *Euclid Avenue Christian Church: The First 150 Years*, 1993, n.p., pp. 52-55; Church Bulletin, 30 June 1946: *Church Life*, 27 December 1947.

56. Dorothy Siegling, *Our 125 Years*, (n.p., 1968), p. 19.

57. *Euclid Avenue Christian Church: The First 150 Years*, p. 52.

58. Fiers, interview, August 16, 1999.

59. "Church Life at the Green Stone Church," Volume I. No. 1, Cleveland, November 16, 1945.

60. Ibid, Volume V. No. 20, January 14, 1950: *Euclid Avenue Christian Church: The First 150 Years*, p. 53.

61. Fiers, interview, July 2, 2000

62. Ibid.

63. *Church Life*, Volume VI. No. 44, June 23, 1951.

64. Ibid.

Chapter Four: President of the UCMS 1951–1964

1. *Indianapolis Star*, 22 June, 1951; *Indianapolis Times,* 8 September, 1951; *Indianapolis Star,* 19 September, 1951; *Indianapolis News,* 21 June 1951.

2. "The Organizational Plan of the UCMS," (pamphlet, n.p., 1950), pp. 1–8.

3. Ibid, pp.1–8.

4. Mark Toulouse, *Joined in Discipleship,* (St. Louis: Chalice Press, 1997), p. 232.

5. A. Dale Fiers to coworkers, 4 September 1951.

6. Virgil Sly, "History of the U.C.M.S: Introduction," (unpublished), 1969, pp. 1, 5.

7. "Philosophy of the United Christian Missionary Society," (Unpublished, n.d.) p. 2.

8. UCMS, "That You May Know," (pamphlet, n.p., 1951), p. 3.

9. "Philosophy of UCMS," p. 1.

10. W.R. Warren, "Survey of Service," (n.p., 1928), p. 13.

11. Philosophy of UCMS, pp. 3, 6; *That You May Know,* pp. 1–16

12. A. Dale Fiers, Interview by D. Cummins, July 2, 2000.

13. A. Dale Fiers, *This is Missions.* (St. Louis: Bethany Press, 1953), pp. 7–11; A. Dale Fiers, "Travel Abroad," *Leaven.* (August,1954), p. 2.

14. A. Dale Fiers to Betty Fiers, October 1951.

15. Fiers, *This is Missions,* p. 26.

16. Ibid, p. 36.

17. Ibid, pp. 62–63.

18. Ibid, p. 70.

19. Ibid, p. 93.

20. Ibid, p. 127.

21. Ibid, p. 76.

22. Ibid, p. 122.

23. Ibid, pp. 123–125.

24. Ibid, p. 130.

25. Ibid, p. 141.

26. Ibid, pp. 144–145.

27. Ibid, pp. 158, 160.

28. Ibid, p. 169.

29. Ibid, pp.165–166.

30. Ibid, p. 177.

31. Ibid, pp. 192–193.

32. A. Dale Fiers to Betty Fiers, January 15, 1952.

33. Fiers, *This is Missions,* p. 245.

34. A. Dale Fiers, "Mission Churches and the Revolution in Missions," *World Call,* (November 1955), pp. 23-26.

35. Ibid.

36. Ibid.

37. A. Dale Fiers, "The Values of Cooperation," (unpublished, undated), pp. 1-6; A. Dale Fiers, "Marks of a Cooperative Church," *Leaven,* (March 1957), p. 1; Alexander Campbell, "Five Arguments for Church Organization," *Millennial Harbinger,* 1842, p. 523.

38. A. Dale Fiers, "This is Big Business," *Minister's Bulletin,* (June 1953), p. 1.

39. A. Dale Fiers, "United Society Revises Plan of Operation," *World Call,* September, 1956: A. Dale Fiers, "How the New Organizational Pattern of the Society Works," *Leaven,* May, 1957.

40. Gertrude Dimke, interview with Harold Watkins, May 2000.

41. A. Dale Fiers, "The Place of Women in the United Society," unpublished address, 26 March 1956, p. 1.

42. Ibid, p. 1.

43. Code of Regulations, UCMS.

44. A. Dale Fiers, "Does the United Society Advocate Open Membership?" *Leaven,* Vol. II, No. 10, April 1955, p. 1.

45. Ibid, p. 2.

46. J. Edward Moseley, "The Christian Church (Disciples of Christ) and Overseas Ministries," in George Beazley, *The Christian Church (Disciples of Christ): An Interpretative Examination in the Cultural Context,* (St. Louis: Bethany Press, 1973), p. 248.

47. Fortieth Annual Report: July 1, 1959 to June 30, 1960, pp. 1-5; A. Dale Fiers, "The Urgencies That Bring Us Together," address to board of managers, June 15, 1960, pp. 1-7.

48. John Fitzgerald Kennedy, *The Burden and the Glory,* (Kennedy Public Addresses), p. 182.

49. Ibid.

50. "Report of the General Policy and Strategy Committee of the National Council of Churches: A Report of the President's Temporary Committee of Six on Race," (unpublished, 1963), pp. 1-5.

51. Gaines M. Cook to international convention member agencies, June 19, 1963.

52. Minutes of the UCMS Board of Trustees, June 19, 1963, pp. 1-2.

53. Ibid.

54. "Principles Involved in the UCMS Involvement in the Emergency Civil Rights Program," (unpublished, 1963), p. 1

55. Fiers, A. Dale, interview by D. Duane Cummins, 2 July 2000; biographical sketch of Elizabeth Kunz Fiers, June 29, 1998.

56. Minutes for the first five meetings of the International Convention's Coordinating Committee on Moral and Civil Rights, June 1963; July 5, 1963; July 29, 1963; September 17, 1963; and October 31, 1963, pp. 1-8; also, the International Convention Coordination Committee for Moral and Civil Rights: Functions and Relationships, September 18, 1963, pp. 1-3.

57. Ibid.

58. Ibid.

59. Staff report to the International Convention Coordinating Committee on Moral and Civil Rights, 20 March, 1964, pp. 1-4.

60. A. Dale Fiers, "Why the United Society Responded," *Leaven,* November 1963, pp. 1-3.

61. Ibid.

62. Ibid.

63. Ibid.

64. A. Dale Fiers, "Beyond Words to Achievement," unpublished sermon, May 15, 1964.

65. A. Dale Fiers, "A Digest of Recent Criticisms of the United Society," 1963, pp.1-3.

66. A. Dale Fiers, testimony on amendments to the Bill of Rights to permit prayer and Bible reading in public schools, H.J. Res. 693, Committee on the Judiciary of the House of Representatives, (June 1964) pp. 2-3.

67. Dimke interview, May, 2000.

68. A. Dale Fiers, "Dimensions of Progress for Disciples," installation address, Detroit Annual Convention, October 1964, p. 7.

69. Alan Fiers, interview by D. Duane Cummins, December 23, 2002.

70. "Some Significant Developments in the United Society during the Presidency of A. Dale Fiers,"(unpublished, 1964); George Earle Owen , "Achievements of Dr. Fiers' Administration," *Leaven,* Vol. XVII, No. 2, September 1964, pp. 1-2.

71. A. Dale Fiers, *Lord, Teach us to Pray.* (Indianapolis: UCMS, 1960), pp. 7, 11, 15

Chapter Five: The Restructure Dream 1964–1973

1. "International Convention of Christian Churches (Disciples of Christ)", unpublished description and history, (Nashville: Disciples of Christ Historical Society, n.d.) p. 1. Hereinafter, references to the historical society will be DCHS.

2. T. J. Liggett, interview by D. Duane Cummins, September 10, 2000.

3. Kenneth L. Teegarden, interview by D. Duane Cummins, May 12, 2000.

4. Joseph Smith, DCHS interview by James Seale, 17 October 1990, p. 1. All DCHS interviews were conducted by Seale.

5. A. Dale Fiers, interview by D. Duane Cummins, November 25, 2002.

6. Herald B. Monroe, "Now He is Our Man," *World Call,* June 28, 1964, pp. 5-6.

7. A. Dale Fiers, "Dimensions of Progress For Disciples," Installation Address, October 4, 1964, Detroit, Michigan, (DCHS archives) pp. 1-12.

8. Ibid, pp. 3-4.

9. Ibid, p. 5.

10. *New English Bible,* I Corinthians 14:26, 39-40.

11. Fiers, installation address, pp. 9-11.

12. *Indianapolis Star,* July 1, 1966; *West Lafayette Journal and Courier,* June 30, 1966; *Dallas Morning News,* September 22, 1966, p. 7C.

13. DeGroot, Alfred, DCHS interview, 10 March 1990, p.1.

14. Teegarden, Kenneth L., DCHS interview, March 9, 1990, p.1; Liggett, T. J., DCHS interview, November 29, 1990, p. 1.

15. Walker, Granville, DCHS interview, March 10, 1990, p. 1; Osborn, Ronald, DCHS interview, May 20, 1990, p.1; Teegarden interview, March 9, 1990, p. 1; Dentler, Howard, DCHS interview, November 19, 1993: Moak, James A., DCHS interview, December 12, 1989, p. 1.

16. Teegarden and Osborn interview; Thomas, Robert, DCHS interview, May 26, 1990. p. 1; Stauffer, Paul, DCHS interview, May 8, 1992; Bayer, Charles, DCHS interview, April 3, 1990; Short, Howard, DCHS interview, July 23, 1990, p. 1.

17. Thomas interview; Bayer interview.

18. Austin, Spencer, DCHS interview, November 14, 1989; Woolfolk, Jean, DCHS interview, March 14, 1990, p. 1.

19. A. Dale Fiers, "Structure—Past, Present, and Future," In George Beazley, *The Christian Church (Disciples of Christ): An Interpretative Examination in the Cultural Context,* (St. Louis: Bethany Press, 1973), pp. 141-167; A. Dale Fiers, "Reflections on Restructure," letter to T. J. Liggett, August 17, 1999, pp. 1-8.

20. Fiers, "Reflections on Restructure," pp 1-4; Fiers, A. Dale, DCHS interview, January 20, 1992.

21. Willard M. Wickizer, "Ideas For Brotherhood Structure." (unpublished address, July 1958), p. 2 ; Robert Friedly and D. Duane Cummins, *The Search for Identity,* (St. Louis: Christian Board of Publication, 1987), pp. 29-30.

22. Ibid.

23. Ibid, p. 3.

24. Ibid.

25. Ibid, p. 4.

26. Ibid, p. 9.

27. A. Dale Fiers, "Our Stewardship as a Council of Agencies," (unpublished address, July 1958), pp.3-4.

28. Tucker and McAllister, *Journey in Faith.* (St. Louis: Bethany Press, 1975), pp. 421, 436-38.

29. Anthony Dunnavant, "Restructure: Four Historical Ideals in the Campbell-Stone Movement and the Development of the Polity of the Christian Church (Disciples of Christ)," Unpublished Ph.D. dissertation, Vanderbilt University, 1984, pp. 393-394.

30. International Convention News Release, August 12, 1964, pp. 1-2; Tucker and McAllister, p. 439.

31. Fiers, "Reflections on Restructure," p. 9.

32. Dunnavant, p. 408-409; D. Duane Cummins, personal reflection.

33. Tucker & McAllister, p. 441.

34. Bayer interview.

35. Robert W. Burns, "A Reaffirmation of Convictions and Concerns," Atlanta Declaration Committee, (Atlanta: n.p., n.d.), pp. 1-7.

36. DCHS interview with Robert W. Burns, November 18, 1989, pp. 1-6.

37. George C. Stuart to A. Dale Fiers, February 1, 1968, pp. 1-5.

38. Dunnavant, pp. 483-555.

39. Fiers, "Reflections on Restructure," pp. 6-8.

40. A. Dale Fiers, "The State of the Church-1968," September 28, 1968, p. 10.

41. DCHS interview with Helen Spaulding, June 28, 1990, p. 4.

42. Virgil A. Sly to A. Dale Fiers, October 22, 1968, p. 1.

43. Teegarden interview, May 12, 2000.

44. Ibid.

45. Fiers, "Reflections on Restructure," p. 9.

46. *Los Angeles Times,* 3 August 1968, p. 9.

47. *Indianapolis Star,* 3 June 1970, p. 8.

48. *Houston Chronicle,* 26 June 1970, p. 6.

49. *Indianapolis News,* 16 October 1971, p. 24.

50. *Indianapolis Recorder,* 13 January 1973, p. 4.

51. Religious News Service, 30 October 1973, p. 13.

52. Howett, Dorothy, interview by D. Duane Cummins, July 16 2000.

Epilogue

1. A. Dale Fiers, interview by D. Duane Cummins, February 18, 2000.

2. Ibid.

3. Ibid.

4. A. Dale Fiers, "The Ground on which we stand is Holy Ground," (unpublished address, October 1992).

5. Betty Fiers, "90 Years: A Great Life-and it's not over yet!" (unpublished manuscript, 1997).

6. A. Dale Fiers, "Called to be a Minister of a Peculiar People," (unpublished address, April 6, 1970).

7. A. Dale Fiers, sermon celebrating fortieth anniversary of ordination, Indianapolis, 1969.

❖ ❖ ❖ ❖ ❖ ❖ ❖ ❖ ❖ ❖ BIBLIOGRAPHY

Interviews

Transcripts of interviews are in the archives of the Disciples of Christ Historical Society.
All interviews by the Disciples of Christ Historical Society were conducted by
James M. Seale at various locations.

Austin, Spencer. By the Disciples Historical Society (DCHS). November 14, 1989

Bayer, Charles. By the DCHS. April 3, 1990

Burns, Robert. By the DCHS. November 18, 1989

DeGroot, Alfred T. By the DCHS. March 10, 1990

Dentler, Howard. By the DCHS. November 19, 1990

Dimke, Gertrude. By the author and Harold R. Watkins. Indianapolis, IN.
    May 15, 2000

Fiers, A. Dale. By the DCHS. Jacksonville, FL. January 20, 1992

———. By the author. Jacksonville, FL. August 16, 1999

———. By the author. Jacksonville, FL. February 18-19, 2000

———. By the author. Jacksonville, FL. July 1-2, 2000

———. By the author. Jacksonville, FL. January 20, 2001

———. By the author. Jacksonville, FL. November 25, 2002

———. By the author. Telephone interview. December 23, 2002

Howett, Dorothy. Telephone, by the author. June 2000.

Liggett, T. J. By the DCHS. November 29, 1990

———. By the author. September 10, 2000

Moak, James A. By the DCHS. December 12, 1989

Osborn, Ronald. By the DCHS. May 20, 1990

Short, Howard. By the DCHS. July 23, 1990

Smith, Joseph. By the DCHS. October 17, 1990

Spaulding, Helen. By the DCHS. June 28, 1990

Stauffer, Paul. By the DCHS. May 8, 1992

Teegarden, Kenneth L. By the DCHS. Dallas, TX. March 9,1990

———. By the author. May 12, 2000

Thomas, Robert. By the DCHS. May 26, 1990

Walker, Granville. By the DCHS. March 10, 1990

Woolfolk, Jean. By the DCHS. March 14, 1990

Correspondence

The Alan Fiers, Furia, and Howett correspondence, author's collection; Kirkpatrick correspondence, Bethany Archives. Weigle, Green, and Goodnight correspondence, collection of A. Dale Fiers; all other correspondence, Fiers Collection in the DCHS.

Cook, Gaines M., to international convention member agencies, June 19, 1963

Fiers, A. Dale to Betty Fiers October 1951; January 1952

———. To coworkers: September 4, 1951

———. To Fellows Overseas: August 16, 1945; June 8, 1942

———. To the author, August 22, 2000

Fiers, Alan to the author, August 22, 2000

Fiers, Leah to Forrest Kirkpatrick: March 27, 1926

Fiers, Russel D. to A. Dale Fiers: July 11, 1991

Furia, Judith [Kankakee County Historical Society] to the author: 29 June 2000

Goldner, Gerould to A. Dale Fiers: August 21, 1945

Goldner, Jacob to A. Dale Fiers: July 25, 1945

Goodnight, Cloyd to Luther Weigle: February 2, 1931

Grubbs, Edward and Jessie to Othel Brown: 1940

Howett, Dorothy [Parkway Christian Church] to the author: July 9, 2000

Green, Irvin T. to Luther Weigle: January 2, 1931

Kirkpatrick, Forrest to A. Dale Fiers: November 28, 1925

McAllister, Lester to D. Duane Cummins, June 14, 2002

Pierson, Darrol [Indiana State Library] to Bethany Archives, May 19, 2000

Sly, Virgil to A. Dale Fiers: October 22, 1968

Stuart, George to A. Dale Fiers: February 1, 1968

Weigle, Luther to A. Dale Fiers: September 23, 1931

Published Works by A. Dale Fiers

Fiers, A. Dale. *The Christian World Mission.* Indianapolis: United Christian Mission Society, 1961.

———. "Does the United Society Advocate Open Membership?" *Leaven* (April 1955)

———. "How the New Organizational Pattern of the Society Works." *Leaven.* (March 1957).

———. *Lord Teach us to Pray.* Indianapolis: UCMS, 1960.

———. "Marks of a Cooperative Church." *Leaven* (March 1957).

———. "Mission Churches and the Revolution in Missions." *World Call* (November 1955).

————. *Prayer, and the Great Decisions of Life*. Indianapolis: UCMS, 1961.

————. *This is Missions*. St. Louis: Bethany Press, 1953.

————. "Structure—Past, Present and Future," in George Beasley, *The Christian Church (Disciples of Christ): An Interpretative Examination in the Cultural Context*. St. Louis: Bethany Press. 1973.

————. "Travel Abroad." *Leaven* (August 1954), p. 2.

————. "Why the United Society Responded." *Leaven* (November 1963)

Unpublished Works by A. Dale Fiers

A. Dale Fiers. "A Biographical Sketch of Alan Dale Fiers." n.d.

————. "A Digest of Criticisms of the United Society." 1963.

————. "Beyond Words to Achievement." 1964.

————. "Called to be a Minister of a Peculiar People." 1970.

————. "Credo." 1933.

————. "Dimensions of Progress for Disciples." 1964.

————. "I remember Palm Beach High School." 1992.

————. "Our Stewardship as a Council of Agencies." 1958.

————. "Reflections on Restructure." 1999.

————. "Reflections on Sixty Years in Ministry." 2000.

————. "Testimony on Amendments to the Bill of Rights." 1964.

————. "The Conflict between Christianity and Gnosticism." 1934.

————. "The Ground on which we stand is Holy Ground." 1992.

————. "The Place of Pastoral Psychology in the Work of Ministry." 1934.

————. "The Place of Women in the United Society." 1956.

————. "The State of the Church-1968." 1968.

————. "The Unified Program and the Local Church." 1934.

————. "The Urgencies that Bring Us Together." 1960.

————. "The Values of Cooperation." n.d.

————. "Westermark's Theory of Ethical Relativity." 1934.

Unpublished Sources

These documents are all on file at the DCHS.

Burns, Robert W. "A Reaffirmation of Convictions and Concerns," Atlanta Declaration Committee, n.d.

"Design of the Christian Church (Disciples of Christ)." Unpublished, n.d.

Dunnavant, Anthony. "Restructure: Four Historical Ideals in the Campbell-Stone Movement." Ph.D. dissertation, Vanderbilt University, 1984.

Fiers, Elizabeth Kunz. "Memories of Childhood and Beyond." December 25, 1991.

————. "Ninety Years: A Great Life—and it's not over yet!" 1997.

Kragenbrink, Kevin R. "Dividing the Disciples: Social, Cultural, and Intellectual Sources of Division in the Disciples of Christ." Ph.D. dissertation, Auburn University, 1996.

North, James B. North. "The Fundamentalist Controversy among the Disciples of Christ 1890-1930." Ph.D. dissertation, University of Illinois, 1973.

Paulsell, William O. "The Disciples of Christ and the Great Depression." Ph.D. dissertation, Vanderbilt University, 1965.

"Philosophy of the United Christian Mission Society," n.d.

"Some Significant Developments in the United Society during the Presidency of A. Dale Fiers."

Sly, Virgil. "History of the UCMS: Introduction." 1969.

Wickizer, Willard M. "Ideas for Brotherhood Structure." 1958.

Books

Bailyn, Bernard. *To Begin the World Anew*. New York: Knopf, 2003.

Bainton, Roland. *Yale and the Ministry*. New York: Harper & Row, 1957.

Beazley, George. *The Christian Church (Disciples of Christ): An Interpretative Examination in the Cultural Context*. St. Louis: Bethany Press, 1973.

Blakemore, William B. *The Renewal of the Churches*. St. Louis: Bethany Press, 1963.

Boring, M. Eugene. *Disciples and the Bible*. St. Louis: Chalice Press, 1997.

Brands, H. W. *The Last Romantic*. New York: Basic Books, 1997.

Camus, Albert. *Lyrical and Critical Essays*. New York: Vintage Books, 1968.

Cherry, Conrad. *Hurrying Toward Zion: University, Divinity Schools & American Protestantism*. Bloomington: Indiana University Press, 1995.

Clark, Kenneth. *Moments of Vision*. New York: HarperCollins, 1982.

Cummins, D. Duane. *A Handbook for Today's Disciples*. St. Louis: Chalice Press, 1991.

————. *The Disciples Colleges: A History*. St. Louis: Chalice Press, 1986.

Curl, W. Donald. *Palm Beach Country*. Palm Beach: Windsor Publications, 1986.

Euclid Avenue Christian Church: The First 150 Years. Cleveland: Euclid Avenue Christian Church, 1993.

Fraser, James. W. *Schooling the Preachers: The Redevelopment of Protestant Theological Education in the United States 1740-1875*. New York: University Press of America, 1988.

Friedly, Robert, and D. Duane Cummins. *The Search for Identity*. St. Louis: Christian Board of Publication Press, 1987.

Furia, Judith. *100 Years in the History of Kankakee*. Kankakee, IL: Kankakee County Historical Society, 1999.

Garrison, William E., and Alfred DeGroot. *The Disciples of Christ: A History*. St. Louis: Bethany Press, 1948, 1958.

Harrell, David. *The Social Sources of Division in the Disciples of Christ 1865-1900*. Atlanta: Atlanta Printing Systems, 1973.

Howard, Robert P. *Illinois: A History of the Prairie State*. Grand Rapids, MI: Eerdman's, 1972.

James, William. *Selected Papers on Philosophy*. London: Everyman's Library, 1917.

Kennedy, John Fitzgerald. *The Burden and the Glory*. New York: HarperCollins, 1965.

Leuchtenberg, William. *Perils of Prosperity*. New York: Macmillan, 1958.

Madison, James H. *The Indiana Way: A State History*. Bloomington: Indiana University Press, 1986.

McAllister, Lester G. *Bethany: The First 150 Years*. Bethany, WV: Bethany College Press, 1991.

Miller, Glenn T. *Piety & Intellect: The Aims and Purposes of Ante-Bellum Theological Education*. Atlanta: Scholars Press, 1990.

Milton, Jay. *History of Jay County, Indiana*. Indianapolis, n.p. 1922.

Morison, Samuel Eliot, Henry Stelle Commager, and William Leuchtenburg. *The Growth of the American Republic. Vol. II*. New York: Oxford University Press, 1980.

Mowry, George E. *The Era of Theodore Roosevelt*. New York: Harper & Row, 1958.

Nolan, Alan T. *The Iron Brigade*. Bloomington: Indiana University Press, 1994.

Osborn, Ronald E. *The Reformation of Tradition*. St. Louis: Bethany Press, 1963.

Pelikan, Jaroslav. *Jesus Through the Centuries*. New Haven, CT: Yale University Press, 1985.

Schlesinger, Arthur, Jr. *The Crises of the Old Order*. New York: Houghton Mifflin, 1957.

Siegling, Dorothy. *Our 125 Years*. Cleveland: n.p., 1968.

Tebeau, Charlton W., and William Marina. *A History of Florida*. Miami: University of Miami Press, 1999.

Toulouse, Mark. *Joined in Discipleship*. St. Louis: Chalice Press, 1997.

Tucker, William, and Lester G. McAllister. *Journey in Faith*. St. Louis: Bethany Press, 1975.

Warren, W.R. *Survey of Service*. Indianapolis: Christian Board of Publication, 1928.

Watkins, T.H. *The Hungry Years*. New York: Holt & Company, 1999.

Whitehead, Alfred North. *Alfred North Whitehead: An Anthology*. New York: Macmillan, 1961.

Wilburn, Ralph G. *The Reconstruction of Theology*. St. Louis: Bethany Press, 1963.

Williams, D. Newell. *A Case Study of Mainstream Protestantism*. St. Louis: Chalice Press, 1991.

―――――. *Ministry Among Disciples: Past, Present, and Future*. St. Louis: Christian Board of Publication.

Wilson, A.N. *God's Funeral*. New York: W. W. Norton & Company, 1999.

Woolery, W.K. *Bethany Years*. Huntington, WV: Standard Publishing, 1941.

Articles

Campbell, Alexander. "Five Arguments for Church Organization." *Millennial Harbinger* (1842).

Fiers, A. Dale. "This is Big Business." *UCMS Minister's Bulletin*. (June 1953).

———. "Travel Abroad." *Leaven* (August 1954).

———. "United Society Revises Plan of Operation." *World Call* (September 1956).

Monroe, Herald B. "Now He is Our Man." *World Call* (June 1964).

Osborn, Ronald E. "The Structure of Cooperation." *Mid-Stream* (December 1962).

———. "The Irony of the Twentieth-Century Christian Church (Disciples of Christ): Making it to the Mainline Just at the Time of Its Disestablishment," *Mid-Stream* (July 1989).

Owen, George Earle. "Achievements of Dr. Fiers' Administration." *Leaven* (September 1964).

Miscellaneous Sources

"Church Life at the Green Stone Church," Volume I, No. 1. (Cleveland, OH: November 16, 1945).

Fiers, A. Dale. Palm Beach High School transcript, 1925.

———. Bethany College transcript, 1928.

———. Yale Divinity School transcript, 1935.

The Bethanian, 1926–1929.

Bethany College Catalog. Bethany, WV: 1925–1926.

Bethany College Class Day Program. Bethany, WV: June 11, 1929.

Bethany College Roster of Students. Bethany, WV: 1928–1929

Bulletin of Yale Divinity School. New Haven, CT. 1933

Bulletin of Yale University. New Haven, CT. 1931–1932

Fiers, Elizabeth Kunz, biographical sketch, June 29, 1998.

Fiers, Russel D. "Fiers Family Newsletter," 3 (October 31, 1992), p.4.

Furia, Judith. "Kankakee History." Kankakee, IL: Kankakee County Historical Society, n.d.

Kankakee City Directories. 1902, 1904, 1909, 1916

Memorial tribute to Leah Honor (Grubbs) Fiers, 1962, p. 1.

Report of the Adjutant General of Indiana, 19th IV, Vol. 4 (186101865), pp. 406–07.

Sports scrapbook kept by Leah Fiers.

U. S. Bureau of the Census. Tenth Census of the United States: 1880 (Illinois). Washington, DC, 1880.

U. S. Bureau of the Census. *Census of the United States:* Washington, D.C., 1900, 1910, 1920.

Year Book and Directory of the Christian Church (Disciples of Christ). Indianapolis, Indiana, 1914, 1917, 1929, 1931, 1935, 1937, 1939, 1945.

Internet Genealogical Sources

19th Regiment Indiana Volunteers. http://19th Indiana.com/19thhist.html

Genforum. http://genforum.genealogy.com/fiers/

Hupmobile. http://clubs.hemnmings.com/hupmobile/history.htm.

Illinois Marriages Index. http//www2.sos.state.il.us/cgi-bin/marriage

K Company, 19th Regiment. http://home.att.net/~b.c.henry/page4.html

Kankakee County History. http://www.prairienet.org/fordiroq/kankakee/history.htm

Kankakee History. http://www.rootsweb.com/~ilkankak/history/k3histo6/k30616a

Kankakee Map. http://tigr.census.gov/cgo-bin/mapsurger?lat=41.11000&lon=87.900

INDEX